My NDE bene

MW01034589

The Near Death Experience of
Michael William AngelOh "0828"

(50th Anniversary Edition)

Second Printing: October 28, 2016

(NDE Anniversary Date: August 28, 1966 / Publication Date: August 28, 2016)

By: **Michael William AngelOh**

ISBN-13: 978-1535458931
ISBN-10: 1535458933

Dedication

I have discovered a true Love beyond all words, as a direct result of my various Near Death Experience (NDE) encounters. Love has been manifested and has personified itself through the enduring relationship I was initially introduced to by my beloved **Mother Olga Iris,** also known to all of us as; **"Mamma Olga".** This transcendental Love was then consummated in Holy Matrimony to my dearly beloved wife and **Lifetime Partner Suzanna AngelOh.** The Unconditional Love, loyalty, support, and daily freely given encouragement I have received from these two most radiant Souls, has been the greatest Gift of **"The Holy Spirit",** I have ever been so mightily blessed to receive in this life. Their Loving devotion is only exceeded by my eternal Loving relationship **with our Lord, Jesus Christ.** These such things, I shall be eternally grateful for throughout this life, and in our Afterlife to come, forever together, and forever all ways.

**"What no eye has seen, what no ear has heard,
and what no human mind has conceived,
the things God has prepared for those who Love him.
These are the things God has revealed to us,
by his Spirit..."**
1 Corinthians 2:9 New International Version (NIV)

Table of Contents

Preface

To you... dear Reader

(The NDE translation of Michael William AngelOh)

Within thirty days of the original publication date of this manuscript on August 28th 2016, I had discovered some previously lost, yet significant details found in my Private Diaries regarding my NDE Storyline which I am now including in the Second Printing of this Book. This would include **twenty-four new paragraph content postings, thirty-six additional paragraph segmentations,** and an embellished **Front Cover and Chapter graphic designs.** I should also explain that I have intentionally capitalized certain words in

1

this manuscript which hold special significance to me and this Storyline. Those selected keywords are as follows; *"The Higher Power"*, *"The Holy Spirit"*, *"The Heaven Seven"*, *"Sacred Heart"*, *"Mother"*, *"Being"*, *"Soul"*, *"Soul Travel"*, *"Thoughts, Words and Deeds"*, *"Afterlife"*, *"Heaven"*, *"Light"*, *"Anniversary"* and of course the names of the *"Creators"*. How did I know the timing for this updated manuscript was right..? This morning on 092816 my wrist watch stopped at **8:28 am**. Good enough for me. My Heart's sincere desire is that the renewed manuscript presented here will be evermore of a mighty blessing to all who journey through this life changing and evolving experience, along with me.

I do not know if the publishing of these manuscripts on the 50th Anniversary of my drowning episode, or **NDE (Near Death Experience)** in **Santa Cruz California** was timed by me unconsciously, or if it's just a coincidence that this year's **50th NDE Anniversary** just happens to be on a Sunday, the same day it occurred, **exactly fifty years ago, to the day.** Perhaps it's simply a piece of the synchronicity puzzle of a larger picture I am not yet fully aware, exists. I'd rather believe however, that it may be a fortuitous destiny whose timing has turned out to be, **as it is.** I do know, publishing my NDE story some fifty years after its occurrence has provided me with a great deal more reflective insight into the meaning of death and my own personal dying experience. Informational wisdom I might not have recognized otherwise if I had published this manuscript in earlier years. During these subsequent years, I've both read and heard of a significant number of other NDE stories. Although they have greatly helped me to understand my own personal experience, I have based the chronicles of my NDE story in this manuscript directly from my own original **Personal Diary postings**. These postings were made long before the word NDE was coined in 1975 in Dr. Raymond Moody's book; "**Life after Life**", and certainly well before I ever knew other NDE stories, were in existence. I had always privately thought that my NDE episode was just my own personal and paranormal experience that no one else would ever understand. Now I know, that supposition was not quite right.

I have had a total of three separate NDE episodes during my lifetime, and I can say that the one I will describe herein had the most significant effect on my daily life, and my personal identity and self-perception. This NDE has caused me to both rethink and rename this experience in more present day terms from what is described as the traditional NDE, to what I would now coin and describe as an; "**RDE**" or a; "**Real Death Experience**". From the exposure I've had with other NDE reports I can safely say my own personal NDE seems to have gone well beyond many of the near death stages I have read about. Ever since my NDE in 1966, I've heard voices and seen visions that might otherwise be considered to be, abnormal. The voices I hear now, sound similar to the voices I had heard during my NDE episode. I can describe them as sounding like multiple primarily feminine voices, speaking together in harmony as one voice. These voices have both high and low range vocal tones and frequencies. At times I hear this group of hushed voices whispering or speaking primarily into my right ear. At other times I will hear them as if they were speaking directly into my mind such as in a thought form, but with the harmonic vocal resonance which I have described.

3

These telepathic transmissions are very different from the usual fifty to sixty thousand thoughts one mind might transmit, during the thought process each and every given day. I can communicate with these Celestial voices by asking a question if I need help with a decision. This is what I have since referred to as the; **"Decision Light Process"**. During this request for help with a question or for counseling guidance, what I also think of as **Prayer**, I will simply sit as quietly and still as I am able for a thirty to sixty-second period. Then I mentally or audibly ask my question, to which an answer or decision may be needed. After posing the question, I focus on **receiving a reply from one or more of my Spiritual Guardians** which can come in the form of an audible response, but in most instances comes mentally or telepathically as a; **"Decision Light Process". My Guardians will use a Green, Yellow, or Red, Light flash of color that they will project within my mind** as a response to my inquiry. **"Green"** means; **Go, or Yes. "Yellow"** means; **Wait, or step back** and **hold off** from making a decision, and **"Red"** means; **Stop, or No,** to the question or decision at hand. In each and every instance I can recall this "Decision Light Process", has resulted in making the correct call and presenting the best answer that was needed at the time, and every time. It is a process I use daily with great confidence, and Peace of Mind.

These voices I commune with on a daily basis, have both faces and personalities connected to them. The reason I know this is because, I was able to meet them in person during my NDE. I was able to hear them and see their faces and so recognized them in the same way, I would recognize a friend or family member. They are quite large in size and seven in number. They have wings and are Beings of the

4

purest radiant Light I have ever seen. I have since come to know these Celestial Beings as my very own; **"Guardian Angels"**. I will describe them in greater detail later in this manuscript, and will be referring to them in these writings as; **"The Heaven Seven"**. For the sake of script continuity, I will continue to refer to this experience as an NDE, even though I will continue to think of it as my own and personal RDE story. I have also been advised by "The Heaven Seven", not to reveal my true physical or personal identity in all matters of external communications. I have not as of this time been told why this has to be as I have asked "The Heaven Seven" the reason for this, and the only answer I have ever received is; **"So be it..."**

There comes a point in everyone's life, where all that truly matters is the healing and harmony of one's entire sense of perception and self-identity. Any contribution to personal transformations experienced, may then evolve. These individual lifetime realizations may then be shared with others as an offering for the possible enlightenment, encouragement, and personal or private metamorphosis in the lives of friends, family, and unknown random others. May you choose this special time with the words, impressions, and images presented herein, to reflect upon the ultimate realities and perceptions you may currently hold, in your own personal lifetime journey. May this manuscript lead to the discovery of your own; **"Reason for Being"**. My Heart's desire for you would be that, in each and every day of your existence, in all of your personal encounters, with all of your relations, through every one of your lifetime experiences, that they may all be blessed by the personal recognition and a more intimate sense of; **"Spiritual Revelation"**. This then is the pledge to life for any Soul, that they depart from this world leaving it off better, than when they had initially arrived on it at birth. May each Soul recognize their own Divine mandate and intimate Spiritual primary directive for Being and **living a life on purpose.** This would include the **relief of suffering** whenever and wherever it is found along the way in life, through the simple daily encounters exchanged with each and every; **Thought, Word,** and **Deed,** while remaining fully focused on one's individual; **"Soul, Role, Goal".** To then leave a campfire of personal discovery and intimate revelations burning for others to see, acknowledge, and utilize on their own **sacred travels along the path of the Spiritual Life,** fulfills one of the primary purposes for existence, as a human Being. This then is the calling I have received some fifty plus years after my NDE. Seems like such a long time ago but then again, it also seems like, **it has been timeless.**

**"The Saints shall exist in the Light of the Sun,
and the elect in the Light of everlasting life,
the days of whose life shall never terminate,
nor shall the days of the Saints be numbered,
who seek for Light,
and obtain righteousness with the Lord of Souls..."**
~Book of Enoch the Prophet 56:3

Introduction

My Reason for Being

(The NDE translation of Michael William AngelOh)

Anyone who knows me recognizes that I simply love Holidays because they provide an occasion to honor and celebrate something or someone that makes everyday life more meaningful, honorable and memorable in living. These are the special qualities and characteristics which turn Holidays, into Holy Days for me. Most Holidays I honor and have written about in my weekly online media publication; **"The Sacred Sunday Journals"**. This publication primarily focuses on American and National Holidays such as; **"Mother's Day, Father's Day, Independence Day, Memorial**

Day, Thanksgiving Day, and **Veterans Day**". Other Holidays I also cherish are celebrated globally such as; "**Christmas, Easter,** and **New Year's Day**". There is however a Holiday I honor each year which is much more intimate in nature, and on which my life has been influenced infinitely greater than any of the other Holidays with the exception of Easter. This Holyday I celebrate as both **a Memorial and Anniversary day.** Although it's not a Holiday posted on the calendar or on which any Local State or Federal offices are closed, it's a day I observe year after year, and celebrate as a day of deeper personal recollection and Spiritual reflection.

On this day my phone, internet, cable TV and e-Mail services may still be active, but go completely unattended. It's a day off from all work as well as a personal disconnection from all my usual worldly duties, social interactions, and pre-scheduled daily occupations and responsibilities. It is a day of **Fasting, Prayer, Meditation, and Silence,** and although the day of the week changes each year, the date is always the same; **August the 28th,** or more simply; **"0828".** This date holds an exceedingly special and personal significance for me because, it commemorates the Anniversary of my "**NDE**" (Near Death Experience) which occurred on an **early Sunday afternoon in 1966** when I **drowned in the Ocean,** directly in front of **the boardwalk, at the beach in Santa Cruz California.** The impact of this day playing in the Ocean as a child continues to directly influence my life in many profound ways up to this very day, some fifty years after its occurrence. It is the central reason I have both considered and decided to publish my **Near Death Experience Story.** I have transcribed this manuscript directly from my own **Personal Diaries,** which entrees have been posted over these many years since the age of nineteen.

This record and recollection of my death and return to this earthly life in 1966, has greatly helped me in promoting a deeper insight and more complete understanding of the daily human experience of life, death, and the process of dying itself. This story represents my own recollected perceptions and personal experiences regarding my transport to a time and place, I have since discovered has been called; **"The After Life"**. My desire then would be that my personal story documented here may also serve as a genuine comfort to others, who may be interested in or may have encountered their own personal NDE, RDE, or **OBE (Out of Body Experience)**. I invite anyone who wishes to honor these Spiritual Realizations and insights, to take a moment at Noon today with a special attention given to Sundays to; **"Light a Candle"**, and take a moment for **"Interior Prayer"**, or **"Personal Reflection"**. Usually my "Interior Prayer Time" is a spontaneous call out for mercy, upon the busy and congestive contents roaming about within my mind. It's my own Heart's call to reveal and develop a purity of Thought, Word and Deed, during the course of daily living. Simply stated this is a time to; **"Quiet the Mind"** and, **"Open the Heart"**. During this **personal Prayer and Contemplative time**, I seek to become more receptive to increasing my attunement to Divine Will, and the revealing of the Divine Plan, pre-designated for my life. My daily prayer time will also include giving Thanks for the many blessings I have received, and for those blessings I may yet be unaware of, having received. I will end my daily Prayer time holding a vision of what has been called; **"The Higher Power"**, **"The Great Spirit"**, or what I prefer to call; **"The Holy Spirit"**. I will bow my head and open my Heart in a receptive mode for the Spiritual insights and guidance I may require in; **"Living my life on purpose"**, each and every day. I will share more details of how to create a proper and receptive atmosphere for developing "Interior Prayer Time" **later in this manuscript.**

On each and every Sunday, which will forever remain my very favorite and most revered day of the week, I will continue to disconnect from all worldly and social interactions. This is the day I reserve for the **lighting of Candles**, focusing on the twinkling of Altar Lights, and the **saying of faith filled Prayers** to; **"The Holy Spirit"**, of **"All that Is"**. I will also focus on my personal Contemplations and Meditations for a deeper understanding of the will of God for my lifetime's journey. On my NDE Anniversary of August 28th each year, I will intensify my **"Prayer and Sacred Time"** to include the practice of floating both face up, and face down, in the Ocean waters and floating within its moving currents. This is the time I reserve for the receiving of **Personal Guidance, Spiritual Visions,** and a more intimate communion with "The Holy Spirit", also known to me as; **"The Comforter"**. "The Holy Spirit" brings a great personal Peace of Mind, Divine inspiration, and personal clarity for my Soul Role Goal's guidance, direction, and my impending reunion with my Guardian Angels, which I will continue to refer to here-in as; "The Heaven Seven". In this Spiritual state of Communion, I will also include a **"Golden Light Visualization"** exercise for Global Harmony along with a sincere Heartfelt Prayer, for an ever growing Well Being and healing of the entire human family. If any of you decide to join me in this Prayer time, then I might suggest if it be possible, that you arrange to take your own scheduled

"**Sacred Time**", to a Natural setting which might include Being at a nearby Park, Lake, or by the Ocean. Being close to any body of water or even in your own backyard, or at some quiet place within your own home, will also do nicely. My hope and prayer is that you may join us as a **member of our Spiritual Family**, as we commune together in the Holy Spirit to fulfill our higher calling in this life, and into the next life, which is eternal.

"Come unto me, all ye that labor and are heavy laden,
and I will give you rest.
Take my yoke upon you, and learn of me;
for I am meek and lowly in heart;
and ye shall find rest unto your souls.
For my yoke is easy, and my burden is Light..."
Matthew 11:28 King James Version (KJV)

Chapter One

My Birth on Earth. The Early Days.

(The NDE translation of Michael William AngelOh)

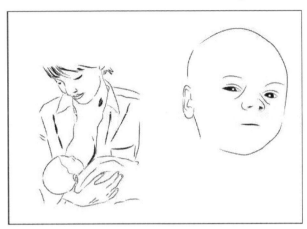

During my early childhood years I had experienced vivid flashbacks of Being wrapped in the fetal position within my Mother's womb, before my birth. These flashbacks would come with waves of warmth accompanied by a Golden Light, which left a deep sense of contentment within my Being by the time of my birth. I can remember Being pulled out of my cozy little womb cave, slapped on the butt, and I could've sworn I heard the Doctor say the words; "**Welcome to earth brother...**" That day in a Chicago Illinois Hospital was; **January 8th, 1952.** One of my earliest recordable memories on earth occurred eleven months later, while I was in **my all-time very favorite place in all the world; My Mother's arms.** The only reason I will share this early lifetime experience is because as I had learned much later in life, this would qualify as my very first discernable **"OBE"** or, **(Out of Body Experience).** This OBE was the pre-requisite for the adjoining NDE episode I would experience as an infant of eleven months old and experience once again, some thirteen years later during my drowning episode as excerpted from my Daily Diary chronicles recorded herein.

I know I was eleven months old, because it was the day my Mother brought my baby brother Dennis home after his birth at the hospital on; **December 23rd**, that same year in **1952**. It was sometime during that day that my beloved Mother was holding and rocking me, as I nursed blissfully in her loving, secure and cradling arms. I recall hearing a loud cry in the distance, Being placed gently down in my baby crib, as I watched my Mother smile lovingly back at me. She then walked slowly out of the room, leaving me behind in my baby crib, and feeling what I would later describe as, a separation from my source of my life sustenance, namely, my Mother. I suddenly felt a shiver of fear and intuitively knew something was wrong. This would be the very first time I had felt such a discontinuous feeling, so deep within the very core of my tiny baby Being. The combination of hearing that cry, which I would later realize came from my newborn baby brother's room, was then followed by the sudden departure from the intimate closeness I had shared with my Mother for some eleven months straight, having been born the eldest and only child present, for all of those eleven months of bliss filled time. As an infant, I had known nothing else than Being held in the nurturing care of my beloved Mother's arms. Now she had left me behind with the root sensation that my newly formed human existence was suddenly Being compromised and coming to an abrupt conclusion. An experience I could only much later cognitively identify as, death or death-like.

This was my first real recollection of a separation from my Mother, someone who represented the source of my very life's essence, existence and sustenance. As I watched her leave my room, I felt like the end of my life had truly come that day. It was as if my life force was departing from my body and was Being removed to an unfamiliar place. Although I still had no cognitive concept of what death was at the time, this was a real experience which in every way, felt like my impending demise which had summoned, my earliest sensations of fear, loss, and impending, non-existence. Deep inside I felt a call, a cry of profound sadness and loss, although I made no audible sound to express this feeling. The intensity of this fear gave way to what I can only now describe as Being, my very **first Near Death Experience**. As I shivered uncontrollably with the ever growing primal fear that an end to my existence had arrived, I suddenly observed and felt a golden Light, begin to glow all around my body and inside my baby bassinette, and continue to expand itself until it filled my entire bedroom. This Light glowed as a bright white orb or sphere, with an intense golden radiant aura, surrounding its outer perimeter. I observed it glowing more intensely in my sudden and stunned state of rapture. This radiant Light continued to grow in its orbital size with each passing moment.

Of course as a baby, I had no idea what was happening. I am now describing it by way of remembrance and in an enhanced retrospect of those passing moments. It was as if someone were turning up an electric dimmer Light switch, but instead of Light bulbs glowing, the Light source appeared to look like **Sunlight filling the room,** to its most luminous capacity. With each and every moment inside this golden Light presence, I suddenly began to feel the deepest sensation of an inner calmness and a profound sense of safety presiding itself, all around and about me. It was just at this moment, I recalled and had seen past images of a very

15

similar feeling, I had once experienced resting within my Mother's womb, prior to my actual birth on earth. The same Light and warmth comforting me some twelve or so months earlier, was again showing that its presence, had never left me. What I experienced next, although it may seem quite unbelievable, felt somehow totally normal and natural to me at the time. As an infant, I had no pre-set mental images or expectations of what was possible or impossible. I saw and experienced a large hand of Light, reaching into my baby crib and lifting my tiny little baby body up, and out of my crib, then transporting me in and through the walls of my bedroom, and through other rooms and walls of the house. It felt as if my physical body were now made up of a **translucency in a body able to penetrate and travel through, solid matter itself.**

I noticed my infant baby body still appeared to be behind me, and resting almost motionless, in my baby crib below. Whatever was happening to me, I discovered later was **known as bi-location.** The ability to be present **in two separate places, at the same time.** It was as if I were **two separate identities existing side by side,** moving in a syncopated motion and **connected by a slim cord or conduit of golden Light.** As my new sense of Being in a Light body was traveling forward, I could see my physical body separating itself from what I had previously thought was me, as I still identified myself to my own physical body. This Light Body which I was incapable of understanding or defining at the time, would later in life become known to me as my; "Soul Body". This newly discovered Soul Body, began its flight moving in and through the walls of the building and infrastructure we would have then called, our home. I say we, because I sensed I was not alone but Being held and

16

transported by this carrier of Light, I couldn't have identified properly at the time but sensed **"It"**, was in some silent form of communication with me. I can identify "It" now, as a circular *Light Orb* which seemed malleable in content, with the ability to morph itself into various forms, as desired.

"It" now carried me forward, passing through the first wall of my bedroom, and then through every wall thereafter, to "It's" desired destination in our home. I was suddenly able to see through other walls in the house and all the way into, the room where I could now see my Mother holding my baby brother Dennis, in her arms. It was within this Soul Body that I had first experienced an existence of a separate reality. I would later discover this new **"Luminous Soul Body"** had its own eyes, ears, mouth, head, hands, arms, torso, legs, and personified sense of Being. This then eventually became my newly appreciated and beloved Soul Body, that was now floating just above and behind my brother and Mother's physical forms, located some four to six feet below my point of visual perception. I felt a great comfort overwhelm me upon seeing my Mother again, as I could plainly observe it was my baby brother Dennis who was in her arms enjoying the same blissful state, I was already so familiar with. Whatever experience of abandonment, fear or even self-perceived death, might have been present within me earlier, now quickly departed from the translucency of my newly discovered; **"Light Body of Being"**. Now was the time I had completely recovered and re-established a total reunion to my Mother's loving presence, within my Being once again. At such a moment perfect peace was restored to me and in the blink of an eye, I suddenly found myself back inside my physical body and inside of my baby crib, as I quietly and quickly, fell into a deep sleep. Only many years later would I be able to understand I had encountered my first; **"Soul Travel Experience"** as an infant, of eleven months of age.

I am often asked why Sundays are so important and so very special to me. It's not an answer I can give quickly or without some deep consideration, because there are so many reasons, **this day is different, from all others.** I suppose it really started back in the early years of my childhood. My beloved Mother was born in Italy, and my hard working and dedicated father was of Irish decent. Both had a devoutly Catholic upbringing which they passed on to us. This meant among other things, we did not eat meat on Fridays, and were raised in a strict Catholic and religious tradition. My understanding as to the reason for this abstinence from eating meat on Fridays, is that it was in remembrance of the day, **Jesus Christ sacrificed his life** on *Good Friday,* for all of humanity. It is then considered to be a form of personal offerings and a day in remembrance of the sacrifice made, by the **Son of God for our redemption** provided lovingly to us by; **God the Father**, whose dwelling place was in our own Celestial Home called Heaven. Our most loving Mother always prepared tasty tuna fish or grilled cheese sandwiches for us on those so-called meatless Fridays, which she carefully packed along with an apple or banana in a brown paper lunch bag for each of us to carry to school each and every day during childhood. I can say I recall many a time where my classmates were bargaining to acquire one of those wonderful sandwiches my Mother had so carefully prepared for us. I don't remember ever trading any of them away to anybody, for anything. My diet has changed quite significantly since those early days. I have been a fairly strict Vegetarian since 1971 when at the age of nineteen, I observed blood percolating out from the top of a piece of meat, cooking on our kitchen stove at home. That very evening at dinner I excused myself from eating the meat, but consumed the tossed salad and baked potatoes instead, and haven't had a bite of meat since. For many years since that bloody revelation, I would fast each Friday from all foods with the exception of fresh fruit or vegetable juices and herbal liquids. It became a day of self-cleansing and dietary purification.

As a good Catholic boy, I was prompted to go to confession on Saturdays, at which time I recall having to make up sins because I usually couldn't remember any of my own. I'm not saying I was an Angel, yet just a very good and usually most obedient child and adolescent. In our family of eight, we all went to Catholic Mass regularly every Sunday morning. I served as an Altar Boy at our Catholic Church; **"Queen of Apostles"**, located in San Jose California. I would so love lighting all the candles before the celebration of each Sunday Mass service. These were all very fine memories, but the most wonderful memory of all was that, after our entire family would come together to attend Mass, we would all file into the families Station Wagon and drive out to continue our Sunday ritual and celebration. This was handled quite nicely with an assortment of jellyroll and maple-bar donuts, along with floating icy chip frosty A&W root beer sodas. After gathering all of our Sunday goodies, we would then drive home. My father would distribute the tasty treats equally to each and every one of us, then attempt to fairly share the comic section of the Sunday morning newspaper. The paper dispersal normally began with me as the eldest, and then circulated down the chronological chain to my dear brothers and sisters. Most Sundays after our morning breakfast was consumed, we would go out for a drive to the nearby Beach, or a State Park. Living in San Jose California, this usually meant going to either; **Vasona Lake in Los Gatos, Big Basin State Park,** or **Santa Cruz Beach and Boardwalk,** all located in Northern California. This combination of childhood events has forever left within me an indelible memory of a loving family, and an endearing celebration of life on each and every Sunday, which I have never since forgotten. This is but one of the many reasons, Sundays became so very special to me as a child. Of course there were certainly many other reasons Sundays became my very favorite day of the week, besides Being the only day I can recall seeing my father, whom I would describe as Being a workaholic throughout my early childhood years. Sundays was the only day I can now remember Being together with the entire Family for at least most of the day. I had already mentioned that it was the day we all went to Mass together and I loved Being at the service, singing the songs and **saying the prayers together as a Family**, with the Church congregation.

When reciting the various prayers said together during the celebration of each Sunday Mass, I had always received mental pictures or images, that went along with the words sung or said, during each prayer. These bright images, shining together with the words of the prayers, made them much more authentic and powerful in their proclamations and devotional intentions for the needs and Spiritual well-Being of all in attendance. These Sundays in the Catholic Church placed me in the presence of the Light, which was shining through the many **stained glass windows**, so prominently placed around and within the interior of the Church. Many times while looking directly into the Light

Being projected through the sacred images portrayed within the sacred glass, I would notice some of the figures begin to move. In some cases, I noticed the Light would project a bright and glowing figure some six to eighteen inches beyond the stained glass surface, making the figure appear to be alive, in more of a holographic form. These Sacred Images moved themselves directly in front of me, and were projected in a most brilliant and vivified Light. The details of the **face and hands of these Holy Personages**, became most conspicuously present to me through all the tiny pieces of colored glass. This was especially the case with the stained glass figures of; *Jesus Christ* and the; *Virgin Mother Mary*. A part of me knew these were only stained glass windows, but I could not deny I was in effect having visions of the Holy Family every time I attended a Church service. I would even on occasion hear members of the Holy Family, Saints, or Apostles present in the stained glass figures, recite the Prayers we were saying together as a congregation. This was just one of the many reasons I so looked forward to going to Mass each and every Sunday morning. I have for some time now referred to this most special of days as; **"Sacred Sunday"**. Years later during my NDE, my most profound experience in the **revelations of my Afterlife**, had shown me very similar figures Being projected in the Light, as I had been so accustomed to seeing in the stained glass window figures, always present to me during the Mass at our Church. What I saw projected in the translucent Light during my NDE, that I hadn't recalled seeing in the sacred glass windows during Mass was, the so-called; **Mansions in Heaven,** which were revealed to me on that Sacred Sunday in 1966 and of which I will always describe as, unforgettable.

Contemplation #01:
"It's Sunday, August the 28ᵗʰ,
a special family outing at the Beach...
Till I stepped into an Ocean undertow,
and was pulled far out of reach..."

Chapter Two

Return to Sender

(The NDE translation of Michael William AngelOh)

I have come to believe there comes a time in every life, when an answer is needed, the unknown is encountered, and a life if it is to continue, depends on somehow receiving an awakening response leading to a life changing revelation in living. Such a time came for me on the afternoon of **Sunday August 28th 1966,** at the Ocean in front of the **Boardwalk, in Santa Cruz California.** After our celebration of Sunday morning Mass, we were informed that we would be travelling to and spending the day at the *Santa Cruz Beach and Boardwalk.* This was one of our Families very favorite places to go on a Sunday morning. Sundays continued to be the one day each week, we could look forward to Being all together and seeing my father, who was usually missing in action during the work week, which went for some twelve to fourteen hours a day from Monday through Saturdays. With our swimsuits already on and cold-cut sandwiches with icy canned sodas already packed, my three brothers, two sisters, Mom and Dad, all positioned ourselves into our families; *1958 red and white Suburban Ford Station Wagon*. We were now ready to begin our highly anticipated Sunday Family adventure together. As always still parked in the driveway, our dear old Dad led us in a; "**Safe Travel Prayer**" consisting of a, "**Hail Mary**", a "**Glory be to the Father**", and his own personal **petition to our Lord for a safe trip.** Then he carefully backed out of the driveway, drove down our neighborhood roadway, and proceeded onto **Junipero Serra Freeway** which eventually turned into Highway-17 heading out for our glorious Family day of fun in the Sun.

Shortly after arriving to Santa Cruz, we stretched out our king size beach sheet on the seashore sand, with the cooler and its ice buried treasured goodies in tow. My brothers and I had always loved to quickly jump into the ocean shortly after our arrival on the Beach, and play a game we aptly called; "**Cutting the Waves**". The object of the game was simply to bounce ourselves up, so as to be able to jump over any oncoming waves while keeping our heads above water. If a wave was such that it exceeded above our head height and our ability to pop up over it, then our backup option would be to simply dive through the Ocean wave and hopefully come up for a breath of air, on the other side. I was the tallest one of my brothers, so I was most qualified to go the furthest out and into the oncoming surf. As we had frolicked together for some thirty minutes or so **playing our Ocean wave game**, I heard my Mother calling us to come in and have one of those wonderful sandwiches, along with a refreshing soda with its sparkling icy cold bubbles which I so loved. As I looked back to the white sheet stretched out upon the beach, I could now see the cooler was already open, and my Mom was pulling out and preparing our sandwiches with napkin placements for each one of us. I **watched my brothers respond to the luncheon call**, as they all headed back into shore, yet I seemed intent and even determined, to remain in the Ocean's rolling surf for just a few more moments to catch another wave or two, before rejoining the rest of my family back on the beach for lunch. Just as this thought was leaving my mind, my next step forward went out, and off, into what I can only describe now, as **stepping off the edge of an underwater cliff**. Beneath my feet no longer was a sandy Ocean bottom, but now only swirling salt waters, as my **body was pulled swiftly downward** and into more powerful Ocean curls and underwater currents.

The water was replete with shuffling mixed sand grains, and further enabled by a powerful undertow. It all happened so suddenly that I didn't even have the chance to take a full breath of air, when I was **yanked downward in a rapid tumbling motion**. I can only describe this experience as feeling much like, Being swirled about in an enormous Oceanic washing machine. I could feel my body moving in and through the strong undercurrents becoming fully submerged, and extended well beyond any sense of personal self-control. What was once just a childhood game, had now suddenly become a serious **life and death struggle for a breath of air, just to stay alive**. I swam as hard and fast as I knew how to get back to the surface of the waters above. I felt my own lungs begin to ache and burn from deep within, as I sharply felt their own craving for just one breath of air.

I'm not sure how much actual real time went by, but it seemed like in my ever-increasing panic I became even more exhausted, as my lungs now began to feel like they might explode from within. As the moments of time seem to be travelling by in an ever increasing slow motion, the Ocean waters provided an ever growing pressure on my need to take, just one more breath of life. I recall intensely hoping and praying that any moment now, I would break up above the surface of the water and be able to do, what I had always been able to do, yet had taken so for granted during the course of my lifetime, and that was, to breathe. Then at a certain moment in my unfolding predicament, a brightly lit image flashed clearly into my mind showing me that my equilibrium had become fully disoriented. What I had once perceived to be my urgent effort to swim upwards, had been turned upside down, and I had actually been **swimming downwards, deeper into the depths of the Ocean waters below.**

It was at this very moment, in witnessing the image of my bodies position caught inside of an insurmountable Ocean depth, that I realized I had no fight left within me. Just when I was convinced my life would soon expire, I observed a **single point of Light flashing** far off in the distance. I was immediately guided to focus on that distant point of Light and in doing so, it grew larger in size as it continued to speedily approach towards me, in an ever growing brilliance. Within moments this Light transformed itself from a distant white dot of Light, into a brightly glowing golden orb of Light, that seem to fully consume me. At such a moment Being fully absorbed into this Light, I presently experienced a deep release of all remaining physical strength along with any fear, I might have had left. I clearly knew there **wasn't**

a single shred of energy left to be found, anywhere within me. Now all the mental survival imagery I once so actively held and projected, simply had nowhere else to go, so it went to a place which stopped everything, from going anywhere. I can only describe this experience in more present day terms by saying it was like; **a computer halt or system crash.** Everything froze on every level of Thinking, Feeling, and Being, which also effectively cleared all of my primordial survival thoughts, concerns and efforts. This then became the moment of my total surrender, which included a clear sweeping away of my life and death's prior operational, survival and preservation instincts. My body and all its internal systems then, seem to become undone and now fully un-functional. I felt I was completely helpless and slipping into a limp state of existence, disabling what was once a viable corporeal reality of my Being. **Such a state of Being,** I had never known or even imagined, was possible before. This internal breakdown or shutdown of all functional life support systems, enveloped my entire Being. Everything I knew or thought to be me, simply expunged itself from reality and into some altered state of non-existence. Perhaps for the first time, I had recognized that my mind had become a total blank and with it, my body became empty of all animating life force and functionality.

As my body continued to be pushed and pulled about into undercurrents of the salty Ocean's water, I seem to have been exported into a very comfortable, lowly lit, **yet glowing and sparkling atmosphere of free floating consciousness.** It felt like I had entered a new room without walls, floors or a ceiling. This room contained such a peaceful and easy state of Being, in which I noticed were some lightly flashing images, shining themselves within the background and in the approaching distance. As I first recognized these images, they immediately drew themselves closer to me, and began morphing into a series of very wide angled and singularly projected shapes. I quickly recognized these projections to be reflections of the person I had once known to be me, during the previous fourteen years of my **collective childhood experiences**. These slideshow type images, now clearly transformed themselves into full three dimensional forms, which appeared to be representing the personalities I had once known to be; **me, myself and I.** These were my own self-created personality characteristics, I had portrayed during my lifetime relationships with family members, relatives, and acquaintances encountered along the journey of my; **"So called Life"**. These images projected themselves in full motion, while others flashed themselves in still or as frozen images in time, like a slideshow continuing to play itself spontaneously before me allowing my attention to objectively observe each projected image, from a distance of self-permeated and un-attached observation. I could feel I was Being drawn into each scenes personal portrayal and depiction of a specific encounter I had experienced during the course of my lifetime, now gone by.

As I watched, I could feel each scene's specific meaning as if my consciousness were Being inserted inside of everyone and every place, Being portrayed and experienced inside of me, and as me. Everything as a human Being I had ever Said, Thought, and Done was now Being projected on a panoramically wide screen, appearing some twelve to fifteen feet in distance before me. This projection screen of glowing Light imagery, wrapped itself in a full circumference all around my sense of self awareness. I felt as if I had become a single entity experiencer living inside all people, places, and things, which I now perceived were wrapping themselves all around me, and as me, in a 360-degree world of projected imagery. The surrounding three dimensional and holographic images were playing themselves in front of me, as well as behind and all about me as if I were inside a large; **"Tubular type Theater"**. It felt like going to the movies, but much more experientially defined and profound because I was now playing within each character's role, and feeling all the dynamics of every life situation as they each unfolded themselves in real time. I clearly recognized this was my lifetime story Being played and portrayed. Just like Being at the movies, I could sense there were others seated or standing close by my current state of awareness who were also watching these projections of my life. I could not see who they were, but I could sense they cared deeply for me and took great interest in this lifetime movie of the life I had lived upon the earth. My previous existence now felt like an open book, Being portrayed for anyone and everyone to observe. There was nothing more to hide and no escape from this projection of my past lifetime's choices, outcomes and occurrences. I would only later discover this experience would be identified as my; **"Lifetime Review"**. It had now begun in earnest, and all I could do was watch as it all unfolded in its fullness of drama.

I witnessed myself as an infant Being born, with the doctor's slap on my backside, resulting in my first cry as my lungs popped open and I took in **my first breath of the earth's atmosphere**. Then a series of childhood memories started to play spontaneously before all watching and present, including my infant *Soul Travel* experience from within my baby crib. This was a moment of intense gratefulness which once again brought me to a deep feeling of interior peace. I would say my Mother was present in most of these lifetime projections, and that they were all deeply nurturing. Then I was transported as a young child of about three years of age, into a highchair seated in the Family kitchen of our warm red bricked home located in Chicago Illinois. There I witnessed myself watching my dear Mother preparing a hot meal over the steaming kitchen stove. I could plainly see I was reaching out with my tiny little arms and hands extended forward, and crying for something my Mother held within her finger tips. For whatever reason I was determined to have what it was she was preparing before me. Upon hearing my continuous cries, she finally relented and handed me the white and circular object. As soon as I beheld the Light juicy orb, I continued to cry as I bit and chewed my way into something I could not as of then, have recognized or properly identified.

I could now see my Mother's face appearing so very surprised, at the spectacle occurring before her very eyes. I could clearly view her face positioned so close and directly in front of mine, as she stared wide-eyed back at me. With tears now freely streaming down my face, my crying continued unabated until my Mother finally recouped the white rounded object from my grasp, and only then did my tears gradually begin to subside. I only discovered some years later in relating the experience to my Mother who confirmed the childhood episode, that this tearful ordeal was initiated by; "A peeled white onion", she was preparing in a tomato sauce that would be served for dinner that evening. Although in the time that has passed since the tearful onion ordeal I had all but forgotten the event, I had developed an aversion to eating any kind of onions ever since. Even at an early age I would ask that onions be excluded from my Mother's wonderful Italian olive oil and red wine vinegar tossed greens and tomato salads. For many years since the onion experience, whenever my Mother asked why I disliked onions I had no rational response I could give except for my saying, I was allergic to onions. The real reason for my aversion only revealed itself many years later during the subsequent reading of my NDE as posted in my **Personal Daily Diary**. I mention this episode because it was just one of the forgotten, yet powerfully influential experiences revealed to me during my NDE, which effected my behavior and the personality traits I would inherit, for the rest of my life up to, this very day.

My lifetime review as such continued to play itself through, with numerous other images of vivid childhood experiences which included personal episodes with my Mother, father, and each member of my family, in turn. As both a witness and experiencer of every past lifetime situation Being projected before me, I was directly inserted into all such encounters which highlighted my own personal behavior patterns toward other people, places, and in all circumstances. All the while the invisible gallery of Beings, who were simply looking on without judgment but with great interest in my story, were always present in close proximity to me. As my lifetime review continued to unfold, I was continually aware of the group of these other viewers watching each and every scene of my life gone by, along with me. Not a single one of the Beings present ever passed any word of condemnation upon me. I knew that the essence of each of these portrayed instances of my life would in turn project and reveal my Heart and mind's true intentions, during the course of my lifetime on earth. There was no place to run and no place to hide, as this little life of mine was Being openly poured out and witnessed by all. The interior intentions of all my; **Thoughts, Words and Deeds,** during my brief lifetime were Being revealed and openly exposed to be either right or wrong, warm or cold, and caring or inconsiderate. I could clearly observe with all others looking on, the moments of my life that had in one way or another caused pain or suffering within myself, or toward another. I felt an immediate and personal conviction of Being in the wrong, if I had caused any level of suffering to any other sentient Being. Conversely, whenever I shared a moment of **Care, Compassion or Kindness** toward myself or another, I felt a spontaneous feeling of joy and Being in the right frame of Spiritual awareness, purpose and function. No one then passed judgment for my life's behavioral choices except, for the all prevailing presence and everlasting Righteousness of; **"The Higher Power"** and their **"Divine Plan"**, for my life.

I became more keenly aware of this Sacred Power and its Presence, within my interior sense of Being. I could feel the essence of this **Transcendental Entity,** engaging itself in all the places and experiences which surrounded me during this display of my personal lifetime's engagements. All of the times I had made the wrong decision in projecting a Thought, Word, or Deed, were punctuated with a clear feeling of Being convicted for my wrong doings. This moment of conviction was then followed by a replay of the same scene over again but this time, reframing my Thoughts, Words and Actions such that my inconsiderate or careless behavior would be revealed, and the correct way of Being under the same circumstances, was then replayed before me as a Life and Love lesson to be learned. In this way, I was Being instructed in recognizing the true purpose of living or what the **American Indians would call living on**; **"The Sacred Path"**. Moment by moment, seeing these life lessons demonstrated, I was able to observe and absorb the truth of how I could have lived my daily life with righteous Thoughts, Words, and Deeds as a human, in all of daily life's situations and circumstances. This process was then a lesson in self-correction toward fulfilling acts of righteousness, or evolving a right Spirit of living a life in harmony and in; **"The Divine Will"**. I now recognized these were the Love and lifelong lessons to be learned as a human Being, during the course of a lifetime on earth. During every episode of my lifetime review, I was now more able to properly correct my wayward Thoughts, Words, and behavior patterns. **My Soul was becoming increasingly cleansed** toward a state of perfection, in its ongoing journey toward purification of purpose, presence and Being. While the flashing images of my lifetime involvements continued to stream by, my personal point of view remained slightly above each scene such that I could easily recognize my face, personal identity, and each involvement on display in each and every one of my lifetime situations. I felt a deep gratefulness from within my Spirit's core, as I continued to experience all such things and register all the collateral involvements, I had caused in every single one of my lifetime events.

Moment by moment as the short story of my life continued to unfold, many loving memories also came forth, primarily involving my beloved Mother as the most predominant influence in my life. There were many other moments in my childhood on the school playground and in my Elementary School classroom where I was now able to witness myself rejecting the friendly advances and encounters of others, due to my own self-imposed desire to be left alone. I had developed a solitary nature I seem to so rigorously need, but which I had never truly understood. At a very early age and perhaps even as an infant, I had always sensed that **I was somehow different** from the other members of our family, as well as other people in general. I somehow intuited I was not properly suited nor would others be able to understand and **properly care for a relationship, with a person like me.** I'm not sure where this belief actually came from although I had known early on in life, that the only person I had ever truly trusted and felt understood me, was my own beloved Mother. And so with this adopted belief I attempted to avoid all such challenging human relationships and potential personal encounters of any kind. It was during these inevitable relationship making moments however, that I was now able to feel the pain and disappointment experienced by others, due to what I was now able to perceive was my own selfish and solitary nature. The desire of others to befriend me and show authentic care for me simply passed me by, due to my lone wolf type status as a person. Up close and personal, I now had the opportunity to correct some of my misguided yet solely self-conceived Thoughts, Words, and behavior patterns that I had unwittingly created as my way of dealing with my life's engagements and circumstances.

As I continue to watch each day of my life unfold, I recall thinking, it was a rather strange earthly existence. My lifetime review continued on as I uncomfortably observed all the many opportunities I had missed, to show care and loving kindness to both myself, and the others whose paths I had crossed. There was a deep sense of sorrow, followed by a need for repentance and forgiveness. In each of these lifetime scenes I could hear myself thinking, I wish I could say; **"*I'm so sorry*"**, to each of these potential friends I had allowed to slip by. These were missed opportunities to show kindness and develop a kindling friendship with the many others, that could have become lifelong relationships, consummated in Love. I was periodically and for just a few moments, left alone in a comfortable darkness after each realization, to reflect on these images and earthly life lessons as they now sunk more deeply into my state of ever expanding consciousness. These then were intentions both inherited and accumulated, along the path of my lifetime. **I do recall feeling a deeper sense of joy** whenever loving memories flashed before me, and then a prevailing sadness when for one reason or another, I had allowed myself, someone else or something else, to stand in the way of reciprocating **"Loving Kindness"** to others. This then was my major takeaway lesson, that every moment of one's existence was a new opportunity to give and receive Love and show Care, or miss the opportunity to do so, because of some self-conceived rational whether done wittingly or unwittingly, during the course of a lifetime.

In one particular scene which seems to stand out beyond the many others, I was an eight-year-old child sitting all alone in what was then called the; **"Tan-bark area"**, located on the playground during school recess. I seemed quite content to be sitting there all by myself. A little boy who was a fellow school classmate walked up to me and asked; **"*Would you like to play ball with us..?*"** **"*No...*"**, I somewhat coldly replied, **"*I want to be left alone...*"** The rejection to my classmate's invitation was immediately evident on the young boy's face. I had not seen it at the time, but now could painfully observe and feel his very personal disappointment even as I viewed the scene unfolding before me. How harsh my response now seemed Being played out on this **wide screen theater of my life** now so openly exposed. I watched in a more sorrow filled state, as my potential playing companion went through his own feelings of rejection and sadly walked away, never to offer the opportunity to connect with me again. I directly felt his personal rejection created by me, and it hurt. Did God or some Celestial representative come down with trumpets of judgment upon me for my own selfish behavior..? No, not at all, yet I immediately recognized the pain I had caused someone else and this in itself, was the judgment upon my actions. It immediately became self-evident and tangibly felt by me, and all those in observance of my actions such that, I felt a sense of shame and sorrowfulness well up from deep within.

All of this exposed before me and all the other observers in attendance, who I already knew recognized the difference between one Being loving, or self-centered in such interactions. Even though I already thought myself to be dead, I was able to **see a bigger picture** in which I was truly only a tiny character in this playground called life. It would ultimately be my own Thoughts, Words and Actions, unfolding within the course of a lifetime which would reveal themselves to be more expansive than my own personal sense of self-identity. I hadn't previously noticed, but my behavior seems to have had a significant influence on so many others during this life of mine, and this made me feel uncomfortable as well. **I realized more clearly now** that the only sense of judgment upon my every Thought, Word and Deed, was if they truly were in alignment with; "**Divine Will**", which permeated it's ever-presence so powerfully in this place of transcendental existence. The presence of Divine Will and their; **"Laws for Life"**, made it quite evident as to what was in alignment with their righteousness, and wrong or in non-alignment, before their everlasting and **"Divine Law"**. I was told that these Laws of Life were founded at the very beginnings of the Creation of the Heavens and the earth. They formed the principals which governed the entire operation of their countless created worlds and Universes. All the many planets and other Universes which existed beyond our earth world, were already in perfect alignment with their Divine Laws of existence. *Was our earth world the only place in the Galaxy out of synch with Divine Will and their Divine Laws for Life..?* I do not know, but all throughout my Lifetime Review I felt a conviction, followed by a sorrowful repentance well up from within me whenever my Thoughts, Words and Deeds caused sorrow or suffering to any other sentient life form. Conversely, beautiful feelings of comfort and joy filled me whenever my Thoughts, Words and Deeds, expressed compassion and care to other fellow life forms.

I knew deep within my new sense of elevated Being, that life was all about aligning oneself to the righteousness of the; **"Creator's Divine Laws"**. Only in this way could one come into alignment with the **Divine Plan that governed all life in its existence everywhere**. Living naturally and **devoted to the Sacred and Supernatural principals** now seemed paramount in the fulfillment of my own lifetime's purpose. Deep within my Heart, I knew the **difference between right and wrong,** and I would strive to please the Higher Power and Holy Spirit, in all my Thoughts, Words and Actions from this moment onwards. I took **a self-actuated oath** to dedicate myself to the obedience and adherence to,

37

their Divine Will and purpose for my life. My Heart would Light up brighter and warmer when I did, said, or thought the right thing, and the same warmth and living Light present within me would grow dimmer, and colder, when I did, said, or thought, in opposition to their Divine Will. This then was the only great judgment, in that no one else had to pass judgment. A self-judgment prevailed as a result of Being exposed to; **"The Divine Law of Love"**, and its natural and supernatural rules for living in a blessed state of Being in their; **"Playground of Life"**. Nothing personal. Pure and simple.

I have heard about and read quite a few NDE stories since my own NDE episode that seem to suggest that no matter one's Deeds, Words, and Thoughts generated during the course of a lifetime gone by, that somehow all would be forgiven or forgotten, when a Soul leaves the body and enters into **"The Divine Presence"** or **Spiritual realms in the Afterlife.** But in this separate reality we call the Afterlife, there exists **a world of Righteousness** beyond any normal or mortal awareness, and worldly human perceptions or comprehensions. It seems it is only through a deficit of personal experience and revelation however, that the idea or belief **that there is no judgment in the Afterlife, can be fabricated.** Precious Souls are misguided and ultimately their destiny will remain in an unclear and confused state, if they insist on proclaiming that the wrong Thoughts, Words and Deeds, transmitted by a Soul during the course of their earthly lives mystically becomes irrelevant in the Afterlife. Also many seem to think that all the misdeeds of an entire lifetime, will somehow be instantly erased by the **Higher Power of all Goodness and Righteousness**, upon a speedy deathbed recantation. I have been shown that the

38

development of a meaningful relationship with "The Holy Spirit" is like a fine wine, which becomes sweeter through time and develops an; **"Aging of Wisdom"**, as part of a lifetime's growing process. The longer a Being does right, or what is pleasing to The Holy Spirit, the more fully that righteousness in Being is rewarded both here, and in the Hereafter. A life lived in greed, selfishness, and with evil thoughts and pursuits then, has its own consequences that cannot be erased by the speaking out of a few words, at the end of a lifetime lived in self-centered goals and pursuits. Preparation for entrance into the Heavenly realms then comes as a result of a life lived in accordance with Divine Law, unless faith is so strong within one's Heart, that it is totally surrendered into the; **"Sacred Heart of the Redeemer"** of all mankind. This kind of faith however usually takes most if not all, of an entire lifetime to consummate.

What other good purpose would there be, for a Soul to go through the trials and tribulations of this earthly life, if it were not for **learning the difference between right and wrong..?** A Soul growing in goodness and righteousness by Thinking, Saying, and Doing the right things for; **"Heaven's Sake"**. Sacred behavior then during the earth life becomes the; **"Soul Role Goal"**, to pleasing the Creators of Heaven and earth. The many other radiant and Heavenly entities that may have once lived as humans upon the earth, also had to endure the many trials and tribulations that we as humans, are presently encountering unto this very day upon this planet. They discovered **a life that was pleasing to the Creators**, and was in perfect harmony with their Divine Plan and Heavenly Will. **Yes, it's true that no one judges us** on the other side we have called the Afterlife, and it is also true, that we do judge ourselves. But what is the standard for this self-judgment..? I submit it comes from the **standards set forth by Divine Law. Like gravity it may be unseen,** but its standards were created as Spiritual principals for the proper operation of the Universe and all its living inhabitants.

These "Divine Principals" are always in force, and act as the everlasting rules which determine what is Divinely accepted as right and wrong throughout all of creation. In humans this sense of Divine Law's guidance in our lives is known as; **"Having a Conscience"**. Like our old friend **Jiminy Cricket saids; "Let your Conscience be your guide"**. We may be encouraged however that they who were onetime human Beings as we are now, do live presently in another world we here on earth, have called Heaven. Yes, there is a judgment of Divine providence as described, and like the so called; **"Laws of Karma"**, there are the seeds of right and wrong that are sown by the individual Soul during his or her earthly lifetime. Each and every Thought, Word, and Deed then, has its own cause and effect, and bears its own individual and well defined fruit. **Do not be deceived then** into then thinking; *"It's all good..."* for even the evil one, dresses up in garments of Light to deceive many. Truly there is a right and a wrong path for living one's life and it is we, who must freely choose the right way back home. Each day **through prayer and supplication to the Divine Will** with the abiding help of; **"The Holy Spirit"**, we may be guided in Love, for Love's sake alone. This is not a need based on Romantic Love, which the material world gives away so freely, but the **Love that is beyond this worlds present comprehension.**

The only way I am currently aware of describing the difference between this Heavenly sphere and this earthly life would be that this Heaven, is the most expansive of all worlds and exists **beyond the 4th dimension, of Time and Space.** This world must therefore be called at minimum, a world which includes and yet is beyond, the 4th dimensional realm of existence. It is a world which exists **outside and above all linear Time and Spatial influences.** This dimensional sphere might be defined as an enclosed capsule containing the all of everything, which has been recorded in the 4th dimension throughout all of time past, present, and in the time yet to come which I have referred to as; **"Time Future".** This would contain the inclusion of all we now know as the entirety of human history, which has unfolded itself inside the parameters of 4th dimensional time and space. From the perspective of the 5th dimension, all of human history could then be watched from its beginnings in Creation, up to its conclusion or so called; **"End of the World"** scenario. To view such a history from the 5th dimension would be much like Being in a movie theater whose attendees **watch the story line of all of human existence.** It has played and been portrayed from its beginning to its timely and destined, end of show. All such things expressed throughout the multiple lives of all the incarnated Souls then, are unfolding their individual storyline existences in and through this dimensional state, we call time.

The entirety of creation's existence could now be viewed from start to finish, by those living beyond the 4th dimension confines, of the time and space package. The books which can be read or viewed as a complete movie as if in a Video Instructional Course, are kept in a Heavenly domain identified to me during my NDE as; "**The Golden Wisdom Temples**". To my great surprise the story of all humanity and its celestially designed conclusion in Heaven, returning its Kingdom back upon the earth, just as the Lord's Prayer states; **"On earth, as it is in Heaven"**, had already been fulfilled and completed. If I had thought of it, I might have found a book in this Golden Wisdom Temple which told the entire story of my own life or any lifetime, I would have desired to look up from its beginning, to its celestial conclusion. I believe here in these Golden Wisdom Temples, is the so called; "**Book of Life**", as described in the Bible. In this Book are the names of all the present and future inhabitants of the Heavenly spheres, which are already written and can be read at will, when once inside and beyond the Heavenly gates.

Finally, after what seemed like an endless period in reviewing my own lifetime events, just as in a theater on earth when the movie ends, there are a few quiet moments of darkness and reflection regarding the movie viewed, or in this case, the lifetime spectacle just observed. So it was for **some silent period of time**, as the silent darkness again returned and enveloped me, that I slipped into a deep and more reflective interior state of Being. Now with a sense of deeper inner peace and contentment, I remained in the position of **Being a third party observer**. My projected lifetime review played itself up and to, the current moment of my fourteen-year-old existence and had projected its final image showing I had drowned, and was still floating under the Ocean waters below. It was precisely at this point that a realization **lit up my Heart and Soul, like a Christmas tree.** I knew now that in this all pervasive Light, there were never any shadows, and that those so called shadows, as identified by humankind and perceived as darkness, were actually only diminished or dimmer quantities of "**Luminous Radiance**" that were always and ever present, which might not otherwise be perceived, in their diminished content of Light. This meant that there was **no such thing as darkness**, and that the so called; **"Shadow of Death" itself, no longer or even ever, existed.** As the Holy Scripture states;

> "Yea, though I walk through the valley
> of the shadow of death,
> I will fear no evil, for thou *art* with me.
> Thy rod and thy staff, they comfort me..."
> *Psalms: 23:4 (KJV)*

Life was always and ever only solely about, how much Love and genuine care was exchanged during all such moments in living. I realized I was now left with more than enough time to process and directly absorb whatever; **"Healing in the Light"**, or corrected perceptions were necessary in order to become a true; **"Child of God"**. More than ever I clearly perceived the originally designed; "Child of God", I was created to be and which would become most pleasing to the Divine. A Higher Power and Holy Spirit who for everlasting life, embodied the **Divine Principals** and **Cosmic Laws**, exposing the **true purpose of all life forms** in existence. My life had now been integrated and aligned with the purpose and everlasting function, of all **Celestial and Heavenly Beings** present, throughout all of creation. Just as there were natural and physical worldly laws such as gravity, there were also Spiritual and Supernatural Laws, and any ignorance or violation of these Laws, carried Divinely created consequences. In this sense the Law itself was the judge, and the violation of these Divine principals would

43

reap the consequences of their adherence, or neglect accordingly.

Auspiciously for me, the loving memories and experiences of my earthly existence far exceeded all others, and I had already at a very early age through the visions of those stained glass sacred encounters, developed a loving devotional relationship with; **"Our Lord, Jesus Christ"**. I was able to complete my lifetime review with a much deeper sense of surrender, appreciation, gratitude, and a true understanding of my Soul's purpose and Well-Being. I experienced the Sacred Presence dwelling within my own ever-living and loving Soul. This Holy Presence was to be treasured and expanded, and then shared with other living Beings which I would encounter along my lifetimes journey. In subsequent years, I have had many flashbacks and dreams of the images and experiences I have described here, during my Afterlife Review. Most of these revelations I have been able to verify had occurred, just as I had seen them Being portrayed to me during my NDE. I now know that whoever I was before my drowning, would not ever Think, Feel, or Be, the same person that dived into the Ocean waves **on that Sunday afternoon.** Perhaps no one on the outside **had ever noticed anything odd about me,** but I would continue to feel quite different, and experience myself as a type of refugee, or foreigner on this earth world. And so this separate and transcendental reality imprinted itself on the deepest levels of my Being from the inside out, each and every day, for the rest of; **"My so called life..."**

Contemplation #02:
"I struggle to breathe,
but no air fills my lungs...
Time stands still, as my life unfolds,
like stepping stones, and ladder rungs..."

Chapter Three

A Separate Reality in my Reunion with "The Heaven Seven"

(The NDE translation of Michael William AngelOh)

Just as my lifetime review had come to its completion, I once again became aware of observing my limp and lifeless body swirling about, and beneath the Ocean currents. At such a time a question formed somewhere inside of my own internal sense of awareness, and my question was; *"How am I able, to see my body..?"* Just as suddenly as my question had formed itself, I heard a nonverbal voice come forth seemingly from within my own sense of interior silence and whisper the answer; *"Not with those eyes, do you see..."* I would describe the voice I heard answering my many questions sounding like **"Multiple Feminine Voices"**, joined together in natural tones with a **"Soft Masculine Overtone**

Voice" resonating around, and over the top of the feminine harmonic voices. I immediately thought, this was not like any voice I had ever heard before. I instantly realized the answer given to me was not referring to the eyes within my physical body, still floating aimlessly some distance away. I again observed my corporeal body which I once was so panicked about rescuing. Now I was watching it, as if I no longer owned it, and now seemingly and somewhat uncaringly was totally detached from its one-time oh so familiar form.

Just at the moment of hearing the answer to my initial inquiry, it suddenly dawned on me, **I have another set of eyes in operation here.** These new eyes seem to possess a whole new and greatly expanded visual perception. These eyes were operational outside and beyond, what I had known to be, my physical body. I recall having once been so fond of using those physical eyes during all those years of my childhood. Now upon clearly hearing this transcendental voice, I recognized the meaning of the answer, **"It"** had given to me. I likewise realized I not only had a different set of eyes, but also a new set of ears as well. Ears which had so clearly heard the soft vocal replies to my heartfelt inquiries which ushered forth so effortlessly, and to my utter amazement. Here I was, watching my body from a distance of some twenty feet away thinking about, then mentally asking a question, then hearing the answers echoing from some place within, yet beyond my internal sense of Being and self-identity. It was clearly an audible answer which I could hear as if someone were speaking directly into my ears, yet simultaneously the voice would resonate within my head like some **"Extra-terrestrial thought form"** that I knew was not my own. What was I to make of this strange out of the physical body, yet more keenly attuned super-sensory experience..? The only thing I could make of it, and that was I had other eyes, ears, sensory units, and even thought forms, which were in operation outside and beyond, my physical form and its attaching brain.

I continued to observe all such things as I became more acutely aware that my new eyes could see in all directions simultaneously. Although I could not presently understand how this could be happening or was even possible, I continued my course of experiencing such paranormal communications with Beings who increasingly seemed to be, ever more familiar to me. I felt I knew them but for some yet unknown reason, I could not clearly place their identities. With my new eyes I could now see much further, more clearly, and with a much greater visual range of everything everywhere than ever before. These newly discovered eyes could see all things preceding me, to the left and right hand sides of me, and most surprisingly, even a clear visual perception of things appearing directly behind me. It felt like having a full 360-degree visual circumference of perception, in every direction. The presence of this highly enhanced visual ability was so expanded, that I was experiencing a sense of freedom, safety, and sensory power, that I had never known before. It was the closest thing to what I might describe as having a Superpower, along with what I would now call a; **"Supernatural Presence in Being"**. One of the most surprising revelations of all was, that I was still breathing. **Yes breathing, under the water**. Inhaling and exhaling some kind of life current moving in, out, and through, this newly discovered Light Body of mine. It was as if I were an open vessel transporting a type of living energy that was contained within the breathing itself, traveling in circular rotations of perfectly concentric and cyclic wave forms, in and through my new and "Luminous Body".

As with breathing upon earth, I did not have to think about **this new underwater breathing** whatsoever. It continued to cycle itself continuously by some unseen force operating spontaneously and automatically, from some place previously hidden deep within me. At this point, I thought to myself in astonishment; *"Am I still breathing..?" "Yes..."* came the answer instantly; *"Always still breathing..."* My immediate response was direct and simple enough; *"I understand..."* At this point I was able to see my arms, hands, and fingers, as they all glowed in a translucent bright white radiance, surrounded by a brightly golden glow. They appeared as if to be formed by sparkling particles of Light in motion, but more concentrated at the very center core of each bodily part's illuminated formation. I was able to continuously see, hear, and think, quite independently from what was once my physical body. By this time, I had forgotten all about my drowning and many of the details of my past existence back on earth. Forgotten all about my onetime intense struggle to emerge from that underwater grave and survive to live on earth another day. Forgotten all about my dying to live, and trying so very hard to take that next breath of life I seem to so desperately need at the time. If anything amazed me it was, that although I was now watching my body from a distance, there was no trace of fear or trepidation about my newly constituted living situation. Now only a feeling of some powerful familiarity remained that I could not have described up to that point in my Afterlife journey. It was only years later that I realized I had been experiencing my second introduction to my Soul

Body, with my first introduction Being at eleven months of age in my baby crib at our Family home, in Chicago Illinois.

All the questions once left unanswered during my childhood, were now Being addressed sequentially each directly in turn, one inquiry at a time, in a way I would describe as Being telepathic. It felt quite natural to allow a stream of all the many unanswered questions that were once so mysterious to me in my previous life, to now bubble up to the surface of my awareness. Now they presented themselves openly and were answered to my complete and fully astounded satisfaction. Answered by the internalized voices which originated from both a place within me, yet far beyond my personal sense of awareness. My total experience of this greatly expanded perception unfolded harmoniously, like some well-timed symphony of Mystical and Spiritual information. This was truly the Golden Wisdom for which I had for so long prayed, and hoped to receive. I intuitively knew I was conducting a higher form of knowledge, from an established source of Transcendental Golden Wisdom. This knowledge entered my Mind like a computer program, uploading itself into the hard drive of my newly forming consciousness, to be used for personal revelation and lifetime application.

Each new thought freely moved through my newly formed; "Mind of Light", at a speed beyond any of my personal or previous comprehensions. At this time, I recall hearing actual audible words spoken and a continuous telepathic transmission, followed by an automatic reception of a new higher form of operational data. It felt like someone whispering quietly but clearly, in a soft and gentle manner. These **"Golden Wisdom Voices"**, embodied a harmony of internal resonance that vastly altered my state of mind and

Being. These were questions I had asked all of my life which had previously received answers like; *"It's a mystery Michael..."* I recognized at some point, these Beings seem to know all of my questions, well before I had thought of asking them. And so it went, with every question and every answer Being exchanged to the point that the process then became automatic. A question would arise, an answer was received, and I recall them following their answers up with comments such as; *"Get it..?"* and I would reply; *"Oh... Now I get it..!"*. Or just after an another answer I would hear them say; *"Do you understand..?"* and I would reply; *"Oh... Now I understand..."* and at other times my reply would be; *"Oh... I never knew that before..."*

I knew there was no question that these Entities could not answer, and so came the final question which was; *"Who is it, that is answering these questions..?"* And with this inquiry, I immediately began to both observe and experience, a circle of brightly lit and self-illuminating Beings, appearing and assembling themselves seemingly out of nowhere directly in front of me, and all around me. They were standing tall in a concentric formation all around and about me. I say Beings because, I could not truly identify any of their specific facial features which is to say, even though I could see they had bodies which included arms, legs, torso and a head, they were covered in what appeared to be, **glowing hooded white robes**. Their faces shining out and through from within their hooded heads in a radiant golden Light, such that no specific facial features could be readily detected. I could not seem to look directly upon them due to the intensity of the Light they projected outwards and into all directions. I do recall thinking while they were circling around me that they appeared to look like;

50

"**Translucent Butterflies with Golden Lighted Wings**", slowly opening and closing the way Butterflies do when they have landed from flight, upon a leaf or flower. I then observed myself standing upright with each of them all assembled together, in a close circular formation all around and about me. From the very beginning of manifesting their appearance, I felt a deep internal sense of the sincerest reverence for them such as I had never experienced before, or since. I can only compare this sensation to an attendance of an ordinary citizen of the earth, Being introduced to the majesty of the Royal Family while shaking in their boots, in an awestruck state of respect and humility. I stood quite still and became increasingly astounded at what I perceived was a highly elevated and evolved presence of; "**Celestial Royalty**". It was this sense of Being in the company of these "**Ascended Beings**", that so touched my Heart, and caused me to gently bow my head in honor with the deepest reverence to their; "**Sacred and Power Filled Presence**".

With my head bowed, and my line of vision also modestly lowered, I was able to lift my gaze just enough to observe that these Beings surrounding me, were quite large in stature. Each Being stood shoulder to shoulder, or should I say wing tip to wing tip, all around me Being some eight to ten feet in height. I was able to count a total of "**Seven Light Bodied Beings**" which with myself present, added to **a total count of eight of us**. They all stood closely together around me as if huddled, just as a Collegiate Sporting Team would huddle together on a field of play. We were gathered in such close proximity to one another, that I felt as if we were all connected together as a single solid unit of consciousness. The Love, Safety, and Compassion I experienced in the presence of these Beings, was incomparable to anything I had ever known at any time leading up to and during, the half century since this mighty **"Celestial Encounter"** occurred. I say this encounter, because although I have had visitations from one or more of these Beings since my NDE, I had not experienced all Seven of them assembled together, as they appeared at this moment in my NDE.

I continued to focus my modest and humble upward glance around the; **"Circle of Seven"**, who had each in turn answered my many questions in life. I noticed a globe of **golden Light circulating around the crown of their heads** like a glowing halo, with a scroll of what appeared to be, some type of character inscriptions. The bright revolving characters were all glowing in a brilliant gold and white lettering. These luminous letters were orbiting or rather spinning, in rotating circles like a kind of; **"Beaming Letter Light Marquee"**. Perhaps these letters were announcing some kind of individual inscriptional identification, or their given; **"Celestial Names"**. Perhaps the orbiting golden letters represented their Heavenly status or the Celestial stature of each assembled Being present. The closest lettering I have seen which compares to these golden glowing images would be the characters I have observed in the **ancient and original Hebrew language.** I could feel each Being's persona striking a deep and familiar chord within me, as if I had suddenly recognized I was in the midst of some **grand Family reunion.** Yes, I would even say it was an experience of discovering long lost and dearly departed; **"Spiritual Family"**. Yet I seemed unable to consciously place any of their identities within my present state of awareness. Just then I observed what appeared to be **a large and gloriously long Banquet Table,** with winged Beings sitting in attendance. A few of those present at the table with its vast ambrosial spread seemed to be looking directly at me as if to say; **"We wait for the day that you will take your place, at our Banquet table here in Heaven with us..."** How I so deeply longed for that day to be this day, but it would have to wait to manifest in its own perfect eternal time and place, and certainly after my earthly duties yet remaining, had been completed. I recall wishing if I could only **speak their names mentally** or **vocally** and **aloud.** Yes I was somewhat surprised to realize, I still had some very strong desires needing to be fulfilled, in this Heavenly place.

As I encountered each radiant Being in turn, I felt as though they were rubbing up against a place so deep inside of me which felt intimate, but which I also had never experienced before. As I presently felt these connections from deep within my Being, they were able to catalyze many profound memories and feelings previously hidden from my awareness altogether. In their presence I felt such a comforting Love, which I can only describe now as Being much like the; **"Unconditional Love that a Mother"**, would have for her infant, or a vulnerable little child. Of course I did recognize such feelings, having had such a strong and deeply loving bond with **my own Mother on earth.** I knew instantly that they knew everything existing within my mind and Heart, including all the shortcomings I had suffered throughout my brief, little existence on the earth. Their **"Unconditional Love"**, superseded anything and everything I had ever thought or could have even imagined, ever existed before. I felt myself **melting into them**, in an ever greater appreciation of their ever expanding Love, all of which seem to be directed toward me, alone.

These then were the radiant Beings, I now knew could answer all of my many most intimate questions in Life. These were the Beings, who rescued me from the fear I had initially felt when drowning and Being unable to take a single breath in that mighty effort to save my own life, back on earth. These were the Beings, who would later in my twenties save me from Being crushed and mangled in two separate car accidents. These were the Beings, who rescued me from the fear of death I experienced so many years earlier in my baby crib, when my beloved Mother left my bedroom nursery, and I had felt so very all alone and abandoned. These were the Beings, who demonstrated and delivered the deepest experience of Love and protection, I had ever or would ever know in this life. These were the Beings, who also seem to know all about my past and present lifetime experiences, and would already know all of my future engagements and lifelong lessons yet to be unraveled and revealed to me. **Were they Omniscient or all Knowing..?**, I do not know, but to this very day I cannot recall the many questions I had once asked, or all the answers, I had so freely received. The dialog shared between us so many years ago still has the most powerful of all influences on my life, up to this very day. Realizations came forth which might have ordinarily taken many days, months, years or perhaps an entire lifetime, to receive and evolve. With a deeper understanding of all such things, I would now observe my lifetime story as it would continue to unfold itself from previous temporal moments, to this everlasting, eternity.

I have for many years since my NDE, continued to refer to these brightly lit and Loving Guardian Beings as; **"The Heaven Seven"**. With all the questions I could possibly think of now answered, and no additional inquiries left or forthcoming, I heard a sound like the thunder of lightning, striking just off to my right side and I began to experience what I can only describe as, an intense inner vibration accompanied by a deeply felt buzzing sound. I then observed the eight of us begin to grow more luminous in our combined radiance. It appeared our Light Forms or Soul Bodies were Being concentrated into an orbital glowing Lightbody, swirling itself outwards from a concentric central core, at incalculable speeds. No longer with a head, arms, hands, or definable torso, our morphing bodies seem to be spinning as the planets would, around the Sun. Perhaps orbiting is a better word to describe this appearance and sensation. Our forward motion at first gradually proceeded onward, then ramped itself up beyond what my words can here-in describe. This was a sense of a quantum speed which propelled all of us forward, leaving a trail much like that of a comet tail behind us, as we proceeded into wide open and stellar space. It took only a few moments before our forward movement accelerated such that things once discernable as Heavenly bodies, such as the stars in the sky, were now passing us by in a blurred state of streaking existence. I had even noticed there were planetary bodies which were now Being left behind in the wake of our brightly streaking trails of golden white, and living Light radiance. If this was the so called **"Tunnel of Light"** that so many other NDE stories speak about, then it was so wide that I could not perceive it as a discernable tunnel as such.

I could clearly see as we proceeded forward, the collapsing of space which once appeared before us, and now quickly disappeared as it folded into a nothingness of silent space, behind us. I glanced backward for a moment and received an observant flashing impression, indicating my physical body was still in floatation mode, down below in the Ocean waters. It was as if my vision were telescopic and that there was no distance between what I could see, and from where I could see it. This vision transformed itself into a view of the entire surface of the earth's bodily existence, as if my vision were Being propelled from everywhere simultaneously, such that I could now view our entire blue world as if it were a picture on a poster, as seen across the bedroom wall, in the world of creative existence. **Now our Orbital shaped bodies** moved directly through numerous banks of floating clouds, and other passing star formations and planetary bodies. The earth became increasingly smaller in size as I continued to observe, the now tiny blue planet begin to disappear altogether, into the distance. Only a brightly sparkling trail of translucent Light preceded our path of forward travel. Something in my experience of both time and space had shifted, and we had now entered into a brilliant window of Light travel, which opened up to a new portal existing in this altogether different dimension of consciousness. My concepts of any chronological order of events had now vanished, and in later reflection I was told that at this point, we had actually **departed the fourth dimension of ordinary time and space**, and had **entered into the fifth dimension or realm of existence.** All my senses were now so greatly expanded in their individual perceptual operations, that they were beyond any description I can come up with to express their transcendental realities. In other words, one would have to be there to understand and properly identify, these Super sensory operations and experiences. At such a point I had thought to myself; *"I wonder where we're going..?"* I suddenly heard rushing sounds like that of large distant and vast Ocean waves, crashing directly in front of us, as one of my "Heaven Seven Guardians" gently whispered; *"Going Home Michael, We're going Home..."*

56

Contemplation #03:
"Slipping under the waves,
then into the deep...
Time to give up the struggle to breathe,
and just go to sleep..."

Chapter Four

My Journey Home to the Heart of the Sun

(The NDE translation of Michael William AngelOh)

Although at no time did "The Heaven Seven" Beings of Light come out and state it openly as such, I have ever since come to know and identify them by name as my very own and ever present; "Guardian Angels". My NDE presented the opportunity to develop an ever expanding and more intimate relationship with each one of them personally. I know now that one of my "Heaven Seven Guardian Angels" did most of the communicating with me during my entire NDE, and told me her name as I could hear her reply directly to my every thought and self-projected inquiry. As I observed those flashing golden characters circling around their heads, like auras or rotating halos of Light, she came forth and stated openly; **"My name is Soularah"**, and after making her sacred name declaration, I heard other voices which were much more subdued and not quite audible to my hearing. And so other names were indeed spoken, yet undiscernible to my current listening abilities. As each of them stated their names though yet inaudible to me, I observed the once foreign inscriptions circling about their heads spell out their names in my own native language of English, which I could now plainly read, one letter at a time. I was now able to see the **characters that spelled out their names**, which continued circulating around and over the top of their heads, as if posted on some type of marquee sign. Just as soon as I completed the reading of each name, the letters reverted back to their original characters which looked like golden emboldened Hieroglyphics. The recollection of the names of "The Heaven Seven" was also removed from my memory, with the exception of my **Guardian Angel; "Soularah"**. I did hear some other semi-audible communications, but they were whispers which I could not make out or properly interpret. As we continued to travel forward, I had barely enough time to realize that we were no longer within the rings of the outer atmospheres, but were now traveling through a **Glorified Space** appearing much like the; **"Aurora Borealis"** in its multiple sequence of colors. Not knowing what to expect at any time along this journey, I now saw a bright circular glowing globe of the most radiant essence and Light source fully radiating before me.

I realized in retrospect, we were in a speedy transport toward what appeared to be the very **"Globe of Light"**, I had once recognized was; **"The Sun It Self"**. A Heavenly Body I had always seen shining so high in the sky above the earth, providing Light and life to our little blue world and indeed to the entire Solar System. I continued to observe the Light World of the Sun expanding before me in stunned amazement, as I along with "The Heaven Seven", continued to streak forward as golden orbs of translucent white and golden edged Light. I could see quite clearly that we were all moving in a steady globular formation, consisting of three Light Orbs proceeding me, one on either side of me, and the other two following closely behind. We continued to proceed in our streaming Light bodies transiting forward toward the; **"Beacon of Light for the Universe"**. All eight of us remained in this closely knit configuration during the remainder of our journey against a background of created matter existing somewhere beyond this place, of deepest space. I recall Being in an altered state of consciousness recognizing that, we were speedily getting ever closer to; **"The Planet of Light"**. At one point I felt a force enveloping all of us which seem to be pulling each of us more directly forward like a powerful tractor beam, originating from the central core of the massive; **"Golden Globed Fire Ball"**, growing ever larger before us. I perceived that our once laser Light speed had now begun to slow down a bit, as we continued to approach the Sun's outward glowing atmospheric halos of golden and white, **"Hot Luminescent Fire"**.

My consciousness was becoming more fully consumed in a transcendental and stunned wonderment, like I had never known, or could have ever imagined existed before. I began to experience a slight trepidation which graduated into an authentic full on fear, about entering the fiery rings and golden flames surrounding the bright, **"Light Planet of the Sun"**. I had always been taught that the rays of the Sun transmitted strong and damaging ultra-violet rays, and I had seen many of my friends and family members burn themselves while basking in, the Sun's warm and radiant Light. I was also instructed in my school classes on earth that the Sun's Light was Being transmitted from some eight-million miles away. I myself recall a time when I unwittingly fell asleep on a sunny Beach on the Northshore of Oahu Hawaii. When I finally reawakened some hours later, I experienced the pain from my crimson skin, having been well cooked and over radiated. The Sunburn lasted for some five to seven days and it hurt even to lay down in my bed, as I had to change sleeping positions from lying on my stomach, to resting on my back numerous times during the night. Even the bed sheets touching my Sunburned skin, gave me a special wakeup call of intense discomfort which I still remember without any special fondness, to this day. These were some of the recollections I was having as we proceeded ever closer in toward the; **"Vast Rings of Solar Fire"**, burning so brightly just before us. It was at such a moment when I was contemplating the possible damage anticipated, in our close proximity to the Sun's Fire, that my fear was instantly delivered when one of "The Heaven Seven" responded to my fear by whispering the words; *"Do not be afraid... This is a fire, that does not burn..."* Upon hearing these words, I most assuredly began to experience a deep sense of inner calmness, and all my fear filled thoughts and survival concerns were immediately assuaged. I discovered then that my faith in "The Heaven Seven" was now absolute, and so we continued our journey forward as we entered what I can only describe as the flaming outer orbital rings, which surrounded the **"Sun's Central Body"**, or core itself.

These rings appeared to be circular like Solar flares, which to my astonishment were not hot, and in fact did not burn, just as one of "The Heaven Seven" Angels had previously advised me. Now, as we had entered and were Being transported through the Sun's glowing outer rings of fire, the circular moving flames began swirling in and throughout, my own Soul Bodies configured form. My every contact with the Solar Flames seem to be transforming the very consistency and cellular make-up, of my Soul Body's substance. I was now experiencing these glowing flames of fire greatly expanding my luminous Soul Body into a more radiant waveform, of living Light particles. I heard what sounded like spinning saucer sounds, whirling all around the eight of us as we continued to slow our progress forward. I immediately felt these swirling orbital sounds reverberating deep within the interior core of my Being and newly vivified **"Spiritual Identity".** These spinning sounds were accompanied by gyrating waves of living Light, forming vast spherical golden globes of the brightest radiance which glowed so brightly all around and about us. **Powerful beaming currents of Light** seemed to be moving in vast magnetic wave formations which captured and carried our Light bodies forward, as if we were surfing on gigantic waves of a; **"Living Light Current".** It was within these awesome **"Waves of Light"** that I became ever more filled with the most satisfying sense of **"Unconditional Love",** such as I had never felt or known before. We were entering into a clearer atmosphere which felt somewhat like a balmy coolness, with gentle winds blowing, and the sweet scent of tropical flowers with their all-pervasive fragrances, lingering within the atmosphere. We continued our transcendental journey together maintaining the same consistent formation we had originally began our travels in.

I spontaneously began to observe many visions of my past memories, of that Celestial body I had always known as, and so called; **"The Sun"**. It became a most pleasant surprise then to discover that although we were moving through many glowing flames of fire, the atmosphere itself was actually very comfortable, and reminded me of the most beautiful day I could have recalled, back on earth. It felt very much like that Sunday afternoon on the beach, at which I could only faintly now, remember drowning at, on this same Sacred Sunday. As we continued our mind altering journey through the many vast circular spheres of golden white Light, we suddenly entered into a large fiery and radiant cloud bank, which fully enveloped and absorbed all of us. Here I felt even a deeper sense of peace, silent majesty, and transcendental tranquility. At this moment I heard one of "The Heaven Seven" say; *"You are in the presence of, the Sun/Son of God..."* When I heard these words although I did not see him directly, I immediately began receiving a vision, of the fiery flames burning within; **"The Sacred Heart of Jesus Christ"**. Of course I didn't know if they meant; **"The Son of God"**, or; **"The Sun of God"**, but I had envisioned the Fiery Sacred Heart none the less. To be clear, I certainly believe that my Catholic/Christian background may well have led to my specified vision of the Sacred Heart of Jesus Christ, but I do also believe that the Love of Jesus Christ extends itself freely to all others who Love God, and that his saving grace is not just for Christians alone, but for everyone. I recognized sometime after my NDE, that I knew without a doubt, that the Lord's own Being and Heavenly residence, must have been in close proximity to this Heavenly region we were presently passing through. My overwhelming sense of reverence and adoration opened itself up from deep within my own Heart, and glowed brightly at the very thought of the words; **"The Sun/Son of God"**. My memory of this moment causes my Heart to grow warm and golden with a transcendental lightness, each and every time I either hear the words or visualize the Sacred Heart, unto this very day. This was an experience of a devotional and indwelling presence which seemed to be coming from everywhere, and from all directions, simultaneously. The presence of all Beings here was fully focused in a deep adoration, which I intuitively recognized some years later was solely directed to the; **"Sacred Heart of the Lord"** and, **"His Holy Family"**. This was surely an experience of the deepest adoration and worship which I had never known before my NDE. I have continued to experience this Loving reverence for "The Sacred Heart of Jesus Christ" and, "The Holy Family of God", within my own Heart and mind, forever since.

As the radiant flames of the Sun's own central fire grew larger and brighter before us, we more closely approached the gigantic center core of living fire, swirling in vast spherical wave formations inside of which I observed were, some type of **"Illuminated Domicile Structures"**. As they first only faintly manifested in the distance, this vision reminded me of what it was once like to fly on a jet plane high over a city and watch the overhead aerial view of the various buildings, except these structures appeared to be designed and assembled together in many various and translucently radiant colors. Each color I observed was Being generated from within each structure, and all surrounded by a brightly glowing and transparent golden Light. As we continued to pass through the multiple large golden rings of glowing white fire, we moved even more closely to what clearly appeared to be numerous communities of; **"Floating**

Light Beings". They were living within and around the Light structures I was now able to see in such bright detail and clarity. Even at our current distance, I was able to observe these **Entities had heads, arms, and legs,** much like a typical human body would possess. I was able to see clear through these luminous forms as I observed a single golden Light shining from within, the very central core of each respective Entity. Some of these Light bodies **had wings as Angels,** while others did not. They all seem to be involved in personally selected and individually desired devotional activities, which they were each expressing, with great Joy. The feeling of their loving presence was palpable, even though I seemed to be such a very long distance away.

Each radiant Being was generating a great devotion and joyfulness, that spun out from within, then directly up and out, into the starry Heavens and toward the **"Creators of Heaven and earth",** who I now knew lived within the central core of; **"The Great Central Sun".** While floating effortlessly above these illuminated domains, I noticed that they were in a **"Dome or Spherical Shape",** and all constructed of Light and translucent type and see through materials. I observed that floating all around us were numerous Dome structures surrounded by other luminous **Light Beings,** who seem to be **playing Musical instruments** such as; **flutes, horns, and many other stringed creations.** Even though many of these brightly lit and circular constructed Dome structures seemed to be many miles apart, the Music created from these seemingly distantly spaced Soul and Angel Entities, all came together as if coming from a singular place, yet their deeply healing and devotional Music was Being projected outwards from everywhere, resonating deeply from within all who were present simultaneously. Their glorious Music was moving in powerful and deep wave formations such that, all sounds were not only heard, but could be seen and felt, in all of their bright and vibrantly living colors. All Beings united and collaborating together in a joy filled harmony, creating a most glorious symphony of Music that filled all of the endless Celestial Space stretched out in its ever-present majesty, all around and about us. I immediately recognized these harmonious sounds could be identified as; **"Worship or Devotional Music"**. I have never heard such beautiful **Heart Opening Music** before, even as a dedicated Composer and Musician myself. I longed ever more deeply to be able to co-create such beautiful Music myself, one day. Along with this **"Transcendental Music"**, I saw other mostly "Winged Beings", singing out in front of their Golden Lit Mansions as their Angelic Voices joined together with the instrumental Music already Being generated, as they combined their glorious vocal chords with the performing Heavenly instruments Being projected into all directions of deepest space. I intuitively knew these Beings were absorbed in the **"Singing of Praises"** to, "The Creators", and "The Holy Family". The closest thing I have ever heard that comes close to describing this Celestial Choral Music would be, soft male and female voices singing; **"Gregorian Chants"**, in a perfect and Celestial harmony.

In other houses or mansions of Light, I saw other "**Glowing Hearted Entities**" all **painting without brushes**, but rather painting with shimmering and luminous colors that proceeded to come forth and out, from the **tips of their fingers**. With a wave of the fingers on a hand, entire streams of the most beautiful and translucently brilliant colors proceeded to come forth onto what appeared to be, vast

"**Artistic Sky Canvases**". These painting surfaces were translucent in texture such that the paintings could be seen directly and straight through, in all of their various vivifying colors and uniquely mostly round and orbital shaped formations. I could only identify a few of the paintings which looked like beautiful Nature scenes of the **Celestial Oceans, Rivers, Floral Valleys** and **Mountains,** which existed here in this infinitely vast and; "**Heavenly Place**". I knew intuitively all such creations here were able to express their deepest gratitude and give Glory to God, for all of the sacred and enduring gifts in creation, **which had never left their spheres of immortality here**. I have never felt a greater Joy than was Being expressed by these Light Beings whether they existed in Soul, or Angelic Bodies, as they collectively filled all the starry depths of space with their everlasting and sacred expressions of praise. I was so very full of Love and gratefulness at this time, that I felt as if I could burst wide open at any given moment. My sense of Being was such that, I felt as if I were Being expanded spontaneously into all directions of vast and everlasting surrounding space. It was truly a deep and an overwhelming Love which now penetrated and permeated, my entire sense of the meaning in; "**Living a Life on Purpose**", or as I like to otherwise say; "**Living your Soul, Role, Goal**".

At the very center core of the Sun, I counted a total of "**Twelve Circular Regions**" or "**Territories of Light**", which appeared to be segmented into individual communities inside of which were, "**Living Light Beings** congregating together. They resembled the communal villages one might see in apartments or condominiums existing back on earth. As we approached ever more closely to the; "**Central Circular Light Orb**" at the very "**Core of the Sun**", I could

68

see within these circular communities were separated Light regions inhabited by numerous Light Bodied citizens. I surmised in later retrospect that these were Souls living together inside of vast orbital communities, as they floated effortlessly about us engaged in their Heaven sent duties all as a unifying and integral part and parcel of the; **"Twelve Outer Spiritual Community Rings"**. Many of these **Light Bodied Entities** appeared to have brightly glowing Wings, and were congregating together toward the innermost four interior **"Light Ringed Circles"** closest to the Central Light Core, of the Sun's Orbital Light Body. Our forward momentum slowed to almost a floating stop, and I felt as if I were on a guided tour Being told telepathically what was happening at each Celestial Scenic Point we had approached, along the way. We did not enter the "Twelve Light Ringed Communities", but now motionless we remained in an observation mode at all that was occurring before us. I felt as if I were witnessing the life cycle of these "Radiant Light Beings", presently so adorned as they celebrated their existence in this most Glorious of all places.

Initially I thought I had noticed some of the Light Beings who were interacting amongst each other, suddenly glance upward and toward my direction. As we continued to hover motionless in the sky above them, they appeared to be waving at me, as if to welcome my arrival. That may have well been the case, but then it became crystal clear that I was observing; **"Choirs of Winged Angels"** within the inner four communal circles, waving their arms and lifting their hands up as they sang in praise and worship together. Their voices projecting forth as if from a single entity and presence of Being. I had never heard any Choir sing as such, that the vibration of their voices shook me with its sonar vibrations, from deep within the core of my own Heart and Being. The **Choral Harmonics** and **Melodious Music** they created together, was unlike any Music or melody I had ever imagined was possible. Their ultra-harmonious singing seemed to be unending, as one group of luminous and Winged Beings moved itself closer to the inner-most rings of **"The Central Sun's Core"**, while another group of un-winged and glowing Beings, took their places. They all appeared to be exchanging positions within the inner-most **"Four Light Community Rings"**, **closest to the Heart of the Sun**. It was as if all living Beings present in this place, only existed to send out praise and glorious declarations outward, and into all directions of Heavenly space, on a perpetual basis.

In this most sacred of places, I experienced an ever-deepening state of blissfulness expanding from deep within, the myriad of Light wave forms and vibrations Being generated all around me. These manifested; **"Sound and Light Wave Formations"**, could be simultaneously heard, felt, and then seen, each in their own beautifully vibrant shades of rainbow colored and misty bright Lights. They seem to appear presently all around me, yet seem to be coming out of nowhere. My Heart was greatly softened, and then melted, as the Love I experienced caused my Heart to grow ever larger in both size and self-perpetuated radiance. I noticed that these Winged Angelic Creatures all circled around some very large Living Entities present, at the "Center of the Sun" on what appeared to be great; **"Golden White Thrones"**, which I am now unable to describe in any perceptive detail. Within the "Twelve Circular Communities of Light", the individual luminous Beings were facing toward the Central Golden Orb present within; **"The Heart of the**

Sun It Self". I have ever since been able to identify this place from Bible scripture as Being called the; **"Throne of God"**. The next thing I saw as we continued to float motionlessly above all we were witnessing I shall never forget. Just beyond the "Central Golden Orb" or "Throne of God", a brilliant and **opalescent Mountain range,** with luminous **glowing Waterfalls** and awesome **flowing Ocean Waters,** surrounded what appeared to be an infinite number of translucent and multi-colored; **"Golden Light Structures".** These buildings glowed like radiation filled Living Entities, and appeared to be the very largest and tallest of any of the Light structures I had seen, during my visit to this Heavenly place. Each structure seemed to be expanding and contracting as if the **"Buildings were each Breathing", such as living Beings within themselves.** The Dome shaped buildings prominently appeared to harbor themselves, within each of the "Twelve Outer Communal Rings of Fire", which defined the various Light Community habitats the Dome Homes existed within. Each Community living within its own autonomous and well defined region. The pure Light radiating forth from this "Central Core of the Sun", I intuitively knew was the source and substance of all Light and Life, that appeared to be coming from within everything in this **"Golden Celestial Wonderland".**

I would later be advised that the manifestation of all creation here, was only possible through the presence of "The Holy Spirit", whose source and **"Immortal Identity"** was generated and known only and exclusively by, the inhabitants or citizens who lived here in Heaven. I now know this place is referred to by all its inhabitants as; **"The Heart of The Great Central Sun"**, otherwise known in Holy Scripture as; **"The Throne of God"**. These radiant Golden

71

Light Estates or Mansions located in the Heart of the Sun, could be seen from everywhere within the twelve surrounding "Communities of Light" simultaneously. Every living Entity from everywhere, no matter where they existed within the "Twelve Circular Communities", was able to face the Golden Throne of God on which I was told that; "**God the Father**", "**God the Son**", "**God The Holy Spirit**", and their immediate "**Holy Family**" were ever-present, and resided. I witnessed countless glowing Souls and Angelic Beings gracefully moving about and attending to what appeared to be, a ceaseless state of loving and life affirming activities, assignments and celebrations. All Beings here which were countless in their numbers, and directed their never ending expressions of glory to God, living within the core of; "**The Great Central Sun**" itself. All Beings present and living in this place were also able to express their own unique forms of glorification, through endless streams of "**Sound and Light Wave Vibrations**". All Light Beings had their hands lifted and waving all about in an upward concentric motion, creating circles or spheres of spinning and massively streaking Light waves, circulating high above their heads. Each golden Being was able to generate what appeared to be, ever expanding Light ripples like may be observed in the stillness of a pond, after a pebble has been dropped into its serene, and motionless surface.

I recall thinking it was as if I was at a Rock Concert on earth, but with hundreds of thousands of Light Beings with their hands lifted high, and shining forth a joy of an all pervasive and thrilling excitement. The Light that this group of Beings created in a single moment could possibly power all the Lights on earth, for many years of time future to come. As we continued to float forward together in this

72

brightly luminous atmosphere, we again were becoming inebriated with all the many pervasive and sweet fragrances that adorned themselves so abundantly from everywhere. They enveloped us much like the **scent of vanilla or amber**, which I had enjoyed so much back on earth. There was no gravity here or as I like to say, it was like Being in a; **"State of Zero Gravity"**. I saw **no signs of aging or disease, no richer or poorer, no lesser or greater, no needy or impoverished**, but only **breathless visions of Light Beings** living in a state of; **"Deathless Delight"**. At some point I became totally transfixed on the vision of a most resplendent and radiant Beach, with golden white sparkling waves splashing in the distance. At my very thought, vision, and desire to visit such a beautiful place, I found myself there, in less than the blink of an eye and transported onto the very beach I had so desired to behold. Now this experience caused me to suspect that **all transportation in this Celestial place occurred, at the speed of thought**. At the very thought or desire, and at the very same speed of instant impressionistic travel, I now rejoined "The Heaven Seven", as they continued to act as my tour guides on this Afterlife adventure. Everywhere I focused my gaze, I observed that all things here were surrounded by **"Radiantly Misting Rainbow Fountains of Light"**, and **"Bountifully Blooming Endless Gardens"** whose flowers appeared to be, individual living Beings who had faces, and also seem to be singing out their joyful presence in adoration, for their very existence in such a place.

These luminous creations of transcendental beauty, seem to be moving in their own loving and living expressions of life wave frequencies. All things I purveyed in this place were so very pleasing to see, touch, and experience, with all my Soul

Bodies newly enhanced senses. They were so very far advanced beyond the senses I had left behind, that I actually caught myself thinking; **"I hope I stay dead"**. Now I started to remember what is was like to live within the confines of the 4th Dimension, back inside of time, and space. The existence in the place I had once lived a life on as a human Being within the **"Gravity Bog"**, on a planet I was already forgetting the name of. It all began to feel like a fading dream that was now quickly disappearing into a silent oblivion. Positioned motionless in the glorious company of my "Heaven Seven Guardians", I began thinking how my life on earth now seemed so much more like the dream, and this new existence was the real and true ultimate reality. Now I was consecrated to simply observe all that was Being presented and unveiled before me, and perhaps I would not have to recall that other rough reality, I had once embraced as my; **"So called Life"** back on the earth. I once again was shown each of the "Twelve Circular and Illuminated Communities", each adorned with its own **defined gardens, rivers, lakes, forests, and Oceans.** How I now longed to live in one of these Communities as they each seem to be moving so very slowly, in their own individual orbits, at their own ultra-gradual and relaxed speeds, yet all connected together and spinning in a perfect harmony, like the planets in our Universe do, on a daily basis. How could I ever forget the **"Central and glowing Golden Orbed Throne of God"**, in the place I now knew and would forever more refer to as; **"The Great Central Sun"**.

Now I was given to observe many "Light filled Bubbles", and circular spheres made from a golden flowing stardust, which were floating freely all around us. Each **"Light filled Bubble Sphere"**, seemed to be fully self-contained with many other Bubbles Spheres existing within, and around each of the "Twelve Community Formations". Within many of these Bubble Orbs appeared to be prominently placed libraries of; **"Golden Glowing Books"**, with illuminated Beings holding these Books within their hands and reading from them directly. I watched in a continuous amazement as many of the luminous inhabitants appeared to be fully absorbed, in the reading and study of these what I was told were called; **"The Golden Books of Wisdom"**, each of which projected its own most radiant Light of wisdom and knowledge. I focused just for a moment on one of the glowing Soul Bodied Entities, as they opened a Book upon which the letters of the words appearing on the page selected, lifted themselves up, and off the page. These Books projected their written characters upwards, above, and directly in front of the page of the golden text that was Being read. The words sparkled into a bright radiance projecting some six to eight inches above the surface of each Books page, as the Soul Entity was fully engaged in reading the contents of the selected script. Each page of the Book turned itself over and unto the next page, so that the reader could continue absorbing its wisdom, in an effortless fashion. I watched just long enough to recognize that "The Golden Books of Wisdom", seem to come alive as if they were, a living entity itself. The Book I was observing turned its own pages, projected its letters, characters and word content upwards, and the Book seem to know within itself, what the reader was absorbing, and when the reader was ready to move onto the next page, for further wisdom transmission and absorption.

As I continued to observe all these things, I was left with a burning desire to hold and read one of those glowing,

"Golden Books of Wisdom", and just as had happened before, in that moment of a thought and desire, I was immediately transported into one of the many Golden Wisdom Libraries, as it beckoned me to come forth and partake of the Golden knowledge held so abundant, within its bindings. Having then arrived, I was able to retrieve one of the many Golden Books from one of numerous shelves, just like pulling a book from a local library shelf back on earth. Now within "The Golden Wisdom Library" itself, I observed that there were many **"Hooded Glowing Entities"**, who appeared to be writing with large feathered pens, like those used to write during the 16th to 18th centuries as was so aptly demonstrated by the Poet and prolific Playwright; **"William Shakespeare"**, or perhaps those ink dipped pens used by the God centered founding fathers, in writing the; **"Constitution of the United States of America"**. I was able to intuit that these were the Authors who wrote Celestial Stories, filling the many Books that were read by all the citizens of Heaven, whose Spiritual Stories inspired an endless and deeper insightful study, regarding the Glory of the Creators and all their Heavenly works. With one of "The Golden Books of Wisdom" now glowing within my hands, it opened its own pages, and the letters and words began illuminating themselves upward, and before my very eyes. Although all of the letters and characters on the page were clear and plain for me to see, I could not recognize the language of the letters or the words posted presently for my preview. One of "The Heaven Seven" sensing my disappointment at my inability to interpret the glowing words of Light, then advised me that, I would be unable to translate the golden text until, I was officially a citizen living in my Heavenly Home. How my Heart then ached to read the meaning of those radiant letters and words, but I understood completely it would have to wait until I became an official resident, of my own Heavenly Mansion. I knew my place in Heaven then, had already been created just for me, my beloved lifetime earth partner, and my Spiritual family members including those who were already dearly departed, as well as all those, still alive upon earth.

This great gift of Golden Wisdom would then be available on an everlasting basis not only to me, but to all those who had left the earth throughout the many past generations, within my own family's long lineage. Each family member progressing at their own time in history, and in their own place of Spiritual growth and Heavenly evolvement. Then unexpectedly in a moment, I was transported out of "The Golden Library of Wisdom", and back into my previous vantage view above the "Twelve Circular Communities" of existing Heavenly Beings. I once again had a floating overview of the countless "Spheres of Light", which remained in their perfectly circular and translucent formations floating effortlessly, through infinite space. As I was in a full concentrated observation, I had remembered thinking; **"I wonder which one of these Spherical Light Domes"** in all of their perpetual morphing transitions, was perhaps; **"My Heavenly Home..?"** No answer came forth from "The Heaven Seven", so I just presumed that none of the Light Spheres I was viewing presently, was my place in Heaven. Then I heard the voice of one of my beloved Heaven Seven Guardian named "Soularah" whisper; **"Don't be concerned my child. Your mansion here in the Heavenly realms, is much more beautiful, than you could ever imagine..."** What a very deep and abiding comfort to my Soul, her comments had made within my ever expanding sense of Being.

Suddenly one of the "Spherical Light Domes" became vast in size and began to look like it might be a; "Celestial Celebrity's Estate". It was certainly much larger and more glorious than any mansion I had ever seen upon the earth. I saw doors opening from the right side of the structure, and Golden Bodied Souls entering as if it were a vehicle, like a Greyhound Bus on earth, only it was vastly larger and made of the purest golden substance. It in fact appeared to be a transportation vehicle into which hundreds of Souls were reclined inside of for a ride, to I know not where. There were vibrant sounds of laughter and celebration however, and again I wanted to join them. In the blink of an eye they were off, and gone. My Heart was by now surely going through a workout of deepest desires, as I wanted to be a part of everything I was observing and experiencing, all around me. Without any notice or pre-meditation on my part, I was now with a group of individual Soul Entities who were emanating great Loving Kindness, and performing many various kinds of **"Devotional Art Forms"**, such as; **Singing, making Music, Painting, and Dancing.** Although each Soul seem to be performing independently, their unique offerings would all join together to the point where, I thought they would become as; **"One Body of Light"**, in their single minded Divine expressions of devotional adoration.

Then again it dawned on me, all of these various Art forms were expressions of perfect devotion, gratefulness and worship. If only the inhabitants on earth could live as they do, here in Heaven. If only suffering earthlings were not Being continuously distracted by the weight of gravity, the daily and unending maintenance of one's physical body, and everything that existed in the material realm, along with the unhappy daily news of worldly affairs, and certainly our own fallen material and monetary desires and shortcomings. At this thought, I felt a great hope in all the many **"Saints and Sages"**, who had incarnated upon the earth throughout time immemorial, with a special devotion to; **"The God of all Creation"** and the Lord, Jesus Christ, and his work of redemption for the entire human family. Then I felt a deep sadness that so many of the inhabitants upon the earth were not grateful for the work of the **"Sacred Ones"**, who had blessed the human race so mightily, and instead so many were allowing themselves to backslide and fall deeper into pride, greed, and meaningless ego-centric selfishness. This was one of the last reflections I would have of life back on earth, as such wonderings would now have seemingly little relevancy, to my current state of ascended mental and Spiritual Well-Being. How very distant those earthly reflections seem to presently be compared to this existence within; **"The Spiritual Sun of God"**. I intuitively knew I had never been or would ever be, closer to the place where the **"Creators and Their Holy Family"** lived in perpetual glory now, and forever more, throughout all eternity.

I continued to walk, or rather float along on sparkling Light particles which themselves traveled within living, self-perpetuating wave formations. The vision of Souls who I later was told were; **"The Saints from earth"**, and the "Winged Beings of Light" I recognized were Angels, never left my state of awareness during my entire visit in these Heavenly realms. Each of them riding Light particle waves, as if they were surfing on sparkling golden Light beams, each ushering them to their own; **"Sacred Heart desired locations"**. As I continued to observe all such things in this suspended state of continuous amazement and super-consciousness, I began to hear a harmonic humming sound that I not only heard, but could feel vibrating from deep within my own Light body and Heart. In the not too far distance I could see other Light Beings heading toward a vast range of Mountains that was surrounded by; **Glowing Crystals,** and **Rolling Gemstone Waterfalls.** Here I saw many other "Golden Citizens" who appeared to be swimming and bathing within the most vibrant and flowing streams of crimson brilliant and shimmering waters. These Beings seem to be bathing themselves inside of the Light filled waters, as if they were purifying themselves, or perhaps baptizing themselves over and again in "The Holy Spirit". I knew by all the humming and happy sounds they generated that each of them was experiencing, a deep and transcendental state of bliss. At the base of these Mountains I could see opalescent glowing Ocean waves rolling gently onto a sparkling white and golden sandy seashore. I heard the gentle roar of the Ocean, whose waves also seemed to be humming in glorious sounds of gratitude simply to be in existence in such a Heavenly place. Each wave carried and was filled with a multitude of various and swimming life forms, celebrating a simple blissfulness for their very presence and Being, in creation. It seemed always and in everyplace that some expression of; **"Praise and Worship",** was the only thing that truly mattered here. **Only Sunday Masses back on earth,** reminded me of these moments of happiness and glory.

As I was given to observe Golden Beings performing on Musical instruments, even inside of and through the many glistening waterfalls, I saw a wall of brightly lit electronic circuits and sliding dials, which reminded me of my own modest Recording Studio I had finally been able to construct along with my Beloved, on my Birthday in 2015, back on earth. Here in this Heavenly World, I was able to envision what truly reflected a future reality of the technical advances I would experience in my own; **"Heavenly Created Media Recording Studio"**. At my intense wondering at all that was now Being shown to me, I suddenly heard one of my "Heaven Seven Guardians" say; *"What you see here, is your own Heavenly Home, awaiting your impending arrival one day... But that day... Is not, this day..."* I felt both a great happiness and a profound sadness simultaneously as I heard these words. Happy to know that such a Heavenly place for offering my own praise and worship Music and Story writing to the Creators and the Holy Family was yet awaiting me, but sad that I would have to wait longer to embrace the reality of its real-time existence. Again I felt my heart strings tugging powerfully at the prospect, of becoming more able to offer all the beautiful Devotional expressions, which lingered so deep and yet hidden, **within my very own "Sacred Heart"**. This was my first hint and indication from my Guardian's statements, that this present day of my Heavenly encounter was a Heavenly glimpse of what was yet to come in my Heavenly Home's timetable, and impending future arrival date. For some reason I unconsciously dismissed and needed to disregard this little clue, that this was to be just a visitation and not a current destination, which I did not wish or allow to register in my waking state consciousness. I suppose this little clue, I had decided to place into a state of denial, because I had been so consumed with such a deep fulfillment of joy, that I wanted to hold onto the thought that, it might never end. I simply wanted to dismiss any other worldly concerns during this long awaited visit Home. **Sadly, I already began yearning for the day** I would be able to return to my Heavenly Home, and recall having the feeling that this day could not come, soon enough. It was at this very moment that a clearer picture that I would soon have to recognize, perhaps sooner than I had thought, and certainly would have wanted, barring any other unforeseen circumstances, would be forthcoming in the timeless moments of my present and future existence. I immediately started to console myself by thinking; **"One day I would not ever have to be leaving my Heavenly Home, for any earthly reason, for Heaven's sake..."**

Now I was back at our original point of suspended reference as if back in the theater, watching a movie, in a separate reality, from a distant world. My sense of profound sadness began to come upon me again at the realization that my stay would be an abbreviated one, and my unwanted departure may well be, arriving shortly. Again I found myself taking comfort in the knowledge that I had embraced a true sense of **"Spiritual Family"** here. I had actually been granted a visit to an assembly of Beings living together within the "Twelve Circular Communities", one of which I myself would be living within as a Heavenly citizen one everlasting day, yet to come. Yes one day I too would become one of these **"Luminous Soul Inhabitants"**, living and devotedly celebrating within one of the "Twelve Celestial Communities" that surrounded the "Home of the Creators", and their Holy Family dwelling within; "The Great Central Sun". I deeply longed to be completely absorbed and fully preoccupied in giving thanks and praise forever and all ways, just like each of the countless celebrated Beings who were living here, but in my own unique and devotional way. My journey's visit wasn't quite over yet, as "The Heaven Seven" reminded me, there were still quite a few more things for me, to see and experience here.

Not only did every Being I saw during my visit have a glowing golden Halo of Light, wrapped and circulating around and above the tops of their heads, but I could also plainly see **each individual Being had their own Radiant Sacred Heart,** with a **white flame** and a **golden aura, so brightly glowing and surrounding, its fiery center.** I noticed that when these Light Beings seemed to breathe, their Hearts were expanding and contracting, accordingly. At the very center of their Hearts, a flame of fire appeared, such that **their breathing expanded its flames intensity,** with each and every breath they took. At one point the flame in one of the Beings Hearts grew so bright and large in intensity, that it seemed to consume the entire Entities body altogether. I was totally transfixed in what I was given to observe, and again felt a burning desire deep within my own Heart to join these entities, inside that **"Holy Fire that did not Burn",** within this **"Sacred Hearts Devotional Domain".** The deep and abiding Love I felt caused me to move ever closer along with my Heaven Seven escorts, toward the very **"Heart of The Great Central Sun".** I am truly trying to describe my experiences here, even though I fully realize that such things are indescribable and well beyond the comprehension of any previous human experiences, abilities, or potential revelations. I began to recollect that even as a small child on earth, I had always **loved the Sun,** it's comforting warmth, and those **wonderful penetrating rays of Sunshine.** The **"Warm and Healing Beams of Sunlight",** entering in and through my skin and bodily tissues, but never, ever, could I have imagined the Sun had an indwelling world of the most transcendental Light, in which was contained a; **"Celestial Civilization of Living Beings".** From a very early age I was taught to say my prayers and yearn to grow in a closeness and **Love for God,** who was described as; **"Our Heavenly Father".** I was familiar with the **Lord's Prayer** and especially the part stating; "**Thy Kingdom come, thy will be done, on earth, as it is in Heaven...**" How I so deeply desired now that this prayer's statements would be manifested, for all my brothers and sisters who were still living, back on the earth.

Now I was in a deep state of internalized reflection regarding the existence of all creation, all originally made in the image of; "**Our Creators**" of Heaven and earth. In this deepest state of Soulful contemplation, I now realized that **having a Father** also had to mean that **a Mother had to be present**, in order to balance and **complete the natural Family equation**. The "**Mother as Creator**", had largely been overlooked, forgotten, and not particularly mentioned anywhere in scripture with the exception of; "**Mother Mary**" Being referred to as; "**The Mother of God**" in Catholicism. I fully recognized that just as a father inferred that a child had been begotten, so a Mother had to be present in order for the father to be recognized, as a father. It wasn't complicated to understand. It simply meant that just as an earthly Mother was necessary to beget a child along with a father in the natural world, so a **Heavenly Father's existence** was predicated on the **existence of a Heavenly Mother in the Supernatural**. This then to me fulfilled the equation; "**As above, so below...**" I realized without a doubt that all of creation was in fact the offspring of both our; "**Mother and Father God**", as our **eternal and Heavenly Parents**.

Now I already know that the belief in a "Maternal Deity" as an integral part of the; "**Personality of Godhead**" or "**The Creators**", may not be in line with traditional Christian teachings and beliefs, but at such times I most usually think of the following statement of Jesus Christ as recorded in Holy Scripture;

"Verily I say unto you, except ye be converted,
and become as little children,
ye shall not enter into the kingdom of Heaven..."
~Matthew 18:3 (KJV)

And I look at it this way. If you believe these words of Jesus Christ you must ask yourself the question; **"Are all the Theosophical points made by folks who interpret the Bible and it's Holy Scriptures understandable by a child..?"** In most cases, it doesn't appear that way to me. Although I read the Holy Bible and find the presence of "The Holy Spirit" and its deep wisdom, can be most often gleaned from many of the words recorded therein, I find that it is much too often used by folks in a way of condemnation that actually turns people off, to ever wanting to know God and their Son, Jesus Christ. **Can a child understand that a Mother would be needed in order to have a Son together with a father..?** Yes, I think so, and so believing in; **"God as Mother"** along with; **"God as Father"**, has been my own personally accepted belief as a **"Child of God"**.

I had always thought even as a child, that this life was about either **getting closer to God, or further away from God,** and their everlasting **"Divine Laws of Life"**. I had now experienced the perfection of these Divine Laws in their Supernatural operation here in Heaven. The Heaven I had always prayed to go to one day, as a child. What I had never realized however, was that this Heavenly place existed within the Heart or core of the Light Planet eternally known to all Celestial Beings as; **"The Great Central Sun"**. Not necessarily the same Sun that we have seen while living on the earth, but just as I was experiencing the counterpart to my human existence in my Afterlife as Being a Soul, so also I recognized the counterpart reality of the physical Sun to be that of a **"Spiritual Sun"**. This Spiritual Sun hovered high above and beyond all of natural creation, shining eternally forth in its Supernatural existence. This World of Light was the beacon of all Light and Life force, for all of existence on earth as well as all the various spinning Planets and Heavenly Bodies, existing throughout our entire Universe. All such things had been created in the image or likeness of our Creators. All things of nature which I had so loved while living on earth had but one major defining difference. The **Sun's Light was shining straight through** and from within every Being, place, and thing here in Heaven, while those same things including all peoples, places, and things upon the earth could be seen only by; **"The Light reflecting off the surfaces"** of their individual life forms. In Heaven then, there were no reflections of Light, just the "Pure Living Light It Self", emanating from within itself, and shining through every life form in its own translucent and everlasting; **"Luminous Presence"**.

Everything seemed to be glowing so brightly within these ripple waves of Sound and Light, all present with the sole purpose of praising our Creators living with their Spiritual Family within this; **"Great Central Sun World"**. Now more than ever I recognized this was a place of learning, growth, and great abiding wisdom, which could be studied and absorbed as an evolvement in developing a Higher Intelligence from within the various; **"Golden Wisdom Temples"**. During my Heavenly visit, I continued to be a witness to both Winged and un-winged Beings, each with their own Divinely inspired personalities and self-generated; **"Soul Role Goals"**. My Being in their presence and my eternal thirst for transcendental knowledge, was then Being revealed and finally quenched. **I recall feeling as if I were**

as a single drop of water, bathed in an entire Ocean of wisdom and understanding. In the company of every single beam of Light, knowing what all Light everywhere realizes which is, that the entirety of all existence was founded on; "**Light and Sound Wave Formations**". I both saw and felt these Sound and Light waves moving in the form of tiny sparkling particles of Light. I was in awe contemplating such things, when the thought I had previously hidden in denial, regarding my visit Being a temporal stay in Heaven, suddenly manifested itself before me, once again. I was certainly more than willing to accept that, I might never have to leave this glorious Heavenly world and that my life on earth, was certainly over by now. But my destiny continued to unfold itself revealing that what I thought, may not exactly be, how things would be working out.

Contemplation #04:
"The Soul travels beyond the earth's atmosphere,
and into the Light...
Dispatching all my doubts and fears,
into flight..."

Chapter Five

My Vision of Decision

(The NDE translation of Michael William AngelOh)
©2016 A Beautiful Dreamer Publication. All Rights Reserved

Finally, having been in a place I now knew to be Heaven, I could see through an endless horizon of; **"Crystal Opalescent Cities of Light"**, all surrounded by countless Angelic and Soul Beings who were all fully preoccupied in; **Writing, Painting, Singing, Dancing,** and generating their never ending Heartfelt tributes in; **"The Healing Arts"**. I was continuously Being bathed and healed by the deepest feelings of their perpetual adoration, leaving me in a bliss filled victorious state of consciousness. These were timeless offerings of worship which purified me, and all things Thought, Said, and Felt within and all around me. It felt very much like I was bathing inside of an endless shower of Light, a perpetual feeling of Being cleansed, purified and rejuvenated, over and over again. I simply never ever, wanted to leave this place I so wished presently to have called my home. I was experiencing Being so very close to the absolute, supreme, and **"Transcendental Magnificence"**, of the **"Almighty Creators"**, and their **"Sacred Divine Plan"** in full flower and operation here. They alone were the sole providers, suppliers and sustainers of all Life in creation, in the Heavens, and on that tiny blue planet called earth. Finally, where all sadness and sorrow were washed clean away, by these endless waves of Everlasting Love and Devotion, my Heart felt only the deepest gratitude, as I continued to float gently and effortlessly along, consumed continuously within glorious streams of internalized gratefulness. One of the most magnificent sights I beheld was the glowing golden white rays of the intricate prismatic designs, created through the awesome and beautiful Sound and Light wave formations. Once again I was transported into all of this glorious Celestial splendor and just for the moment, I had totally forgotten all about the perpetual mellow dramas that were still most likely happening, back on earth.

I affirmed I could not ever imagine finding any reason to ever leave this place. As this very thought crossed my mind, a short series of images began flashing across the wider screen of my consciousness. They managed to suspend my present state of blissful awareness. In the background I was still ever aware of the most Transcendental Peace and Happiness, I had ever known. Even as I had thought the movie review of my past life in earth time had surely ended, I now began receiving newly transmitted images portending a possible projected future of friends and family, who would be attending the funeral of a fourteen-year old child, who had drowned at a Sunday family picnic on the beach, in Santa Cruz California. I was witnessing a projection of my own open face casket, seeing my body resting inside the silken white laced container with a Holy Rosary, grasped within and between my prayerfully arranged fingers. This is the Catholic way to honor and celebrate a Funeral service. The potential result of my sudden absence from earthly life was now Being demonstrated directly in front of me in vivid detail. I actually felt I was in attendance with my immediate family, friends, and relatives, at my own Memorial. I was made then to recognize that my absence from life on earth, was resulting in the Heart wrenching sobs of my beloved Mother, who was surrounded by our family all grieving together, in the funeral chapel. She was Being held up in my father's arms as if she were unable to stand or even sit up, on her own. My beloved brothers and sisters were surrounding our Mother, trying their very best to console her, in her broken state of Being. Upon my observance of this scene of pain filled tragedy, I needed no one to tell me that my death and funeral were having devastating effects on my dearly beloved Mother's Heart. I knew now that her life in the coming days, months, and years, could never and would ever, be the same again. It became all too apparent to me that the Mother I had come to know and Love so deeply, Being her first born on earth, would now not be the same Mother I had known growing up, during my childhood. This intense pain and grief only existed as a direct result of my physical absence, due to a tragedy which caused an irreparable damage of guilt and pain, for the remainder of my Mother's lifetime on earth.

The tragedy of my death would change the nature and identity of my Mother's personality, as well as affect the course of her involvement in all her relationships, to every member in our Family. From the day of my drowning on August 28th, going forth throughout the remaining days in her life, this pain my beloved Mother experienced now became my pain as well. It was a very personal and devastating guilt, coupled with the deepest sorrow I had ever known, breaking my Mother's Heart even as it was now, fracturing my own Heart. I watched intently as my Mother became increasingly convinced of her own failure to protect her eldest little boy's life in the water, on that tragic day in August. It was only supposed to be a Family's picnic reveling upon the beach. Now I was shown a time future period which was speeded up and revealed, that my beloved Mother had continued to carry an ongoing and perpetual crushing remorse, which would not diminish over time. This grief spread like some kind of disease within my Mother's beautiful Soul, from day to day. I wondered if her heartache would ever end, or if like some poisonous substance, it would culminate in her aging more rapidly and end ultimately, in her untimely death. I now recognized that this tragedy of my formerly bliss filled Heaven sent existence, could now seriously impair my Mother's ability to carry on in fulfilling, her Motherhood duties in life. How could she then properly care for and Love my beloved brothers and sisters..? How would she fulfill her pledged partnership role, to my dear and hardworking father..? In other words, how would she be able to go forth in her life on earth, with this crushing weight around her Heart and Soul..?

I was required to witness and understand the consequences of a decision, that I was now faced with having to make. This decision would affect the rest of my Mother's life, as well as the outcome of my entire family's individual, and personal experiences for the rest of their lifetimes. I had never before realized how important a single decision could be. This moment would determine the outcome of life, for many others involved in their individual dramas and lifetime lessons on earth. I believed "The Heaven Seven" to be, my own devoted and designated Guardian Angels, and on this thought they all appeared to help guide me in making this life altering decision. I trembled just a bit at the awesome implications of my decision now at hand, waiting to be consummated and so set forth in eternity. I also recognized I was at a point where, if I had travelled any further forward into my Heavenly experience, I would be beyond a point, of no return, back to my earthly existence. Once I realized the unimaginable devastating influence and ultra-challenging hardships my earthly departure would have on my Mother and our entire family, I knew I had to stop my newly discovered Life in Heaven, immediately in its tracks. The options I might have to make regarding this decision might otherwise and shortly become, totally unavailable to me. I replayed the future visions and the profound consequences now realizing the outcome my decision would have, on all such things. My potential absence from earth life affecting all those I most Loved, I now had already decided, was unacceptable. These tragic future events became much too compelling for my own Heart and Soul to endure, even for another moment. Now I began bargaining for how I might arrange for my return back to my prior earth life, with "The Heaven Seven", by my side.

Without my having to say anything about what I was thinking or feeling, my "Heaven Seven Guardians" reassembled themselves in a complete circular formation all around me, as they had done at the beginning of this journey. A telepathic transfer of my possible return options began projecting themselves before me. Their silent but clear visionary communications opened themselves up from within me. My Guardians knew better than I, what options I had available. They already knew all of the implications of the choice I would have to make. Collectively, they began projecting images of how it would all work out and what it would all mean to me, if I continued my existence back on earth. The very first thing "The Heaven Seven" helped me to recognize was, that with all the Celestial and Heavenly visions in Being I had already absorbed, my return to earth certainly could be arranged, but the change in plans at this point in my Afterlife, would be neither easy nor should be taken lightly. There would be many extenuating consequences in store for me once my return was granted, and arranged. I asked no further questions at this point but remained silent. I simply listened with the deepest concentration and reverence I could muster on "The Heaven Seven's" image communications, now Being telepathically transmitted to me. The future effects on my life as it would be back on earth, and its outcome on all the other Love lessons and the relationships that were yet to be developed with many other Loving Souls, I had not even met or come to know yet. These were Souls who would be entering into my future existence during my extended life now Being requested, upon the earth. As it turns out now, fifty years of Love Lessons later, the most beautiful relationships I could have never imagined were yet awaiting to engage me, including the meeting of my Soul Mate and Life time partner. These relationships or as my American Indian friends would say; **"All my Relations"**, would now be included in my time future experiences all yet unknown to me, at fourteen-years

94

of age. The main concerning issues "The Heaven Seven" had showed me seemed to be, how I would be able to reconcile my other-worldly experiences I had already encountered here, in the Celestial and Heavenly Worlds. How would I now, be able to relate such transcendental experiences, **in a life recommitted as a human Being..?** I had been living for such a timeless period in a; **"State of Zero Gravity"**, and now I would be returning to the "Gravitational Bog" of a life, on earth. The experience of my impending return would result in my having to become a somebody, in a very different world than the Heavenly existence I was quite content to remain in on an eternal basis. I had already been experiencing a very different atmosphere of awareness and presence in Being. How would I now be able to reconcile my Souls transfer back into my much more densely packed and corporeal life form..? I, as a Soul Entity, did not presently know the answer to this formidable question.

One of the last things I would have to seriously consider was, how I would deal with the dense gravitational field with all of its inertia, which I had not had to contend with living outside of, time and space. This then became the ultimate reality of having experienced Heaven in all its glory, and now coming to grips with leaving it all behind and returning to the grind of pushing that physical body around and about, all over again. I would have to somehow reconcile these many differences in existence between these two separate realities. I would have to walk the line of having new and profound memories between these two markedly different lives, in these two vastly different worlds. I recognized even after all the projected struggles I would be facing, that I was somehow already pre-destined to make this choice, primarily for my Mother's sake. I would have to leave all the details for the arrangements necessary to ensure my return back to earth, to my enduring faith in; "My Heaven Seven Guardians". I was in a deep surrender mode, totally dependent on their help in guiding me at this point. Before I could say or think anything differently about the subject, "The Heaven Seven" had already completed the plans and all the arrangements necessary for my re-entry as I heard them say; *"Some of what you have seen, learned, and experienced here, will be removed from your memory..."* I silently acknowledged this communication and nodded my head in agreement. The last thing I can recall them telling me was; *"Do not be afraid, we will always, be with you..."* I silently nodded my head again, giving them a smile of heartfelt gratitude for all their Loving guidance and the abiding care they had showered upon me, in this unforgettable journey and timeless visit to my Heavenly Home.

Then, without any further notice or communication from them, I experienced a transfer of my **Soul's Light Body,** in less than the blink of an eye. I immediately felt like a cold, lifeless hunk of seaweed, which turned out to be a trace of re-awareness in my return into that wavering physical body **still floating aimlessly, beneath the Sea**. I suddenly felt heavily burdened by the weight and density inside of my physical body, feeling much like Being within a balloon filled with molten lead, and sunken to the bottom of the Ocean. Strong feelings of grief, loss, and trepidation filled me, as I truly did not know what was to become of me. At such a moment I experienced a deep warming glow, as if a pocket heater had been ignited within my Heart, and I immediately knew, my "Heaven Seven Angelic Guardians" were with me, once again. Now in a deep heartfelt gratefulness, my faith increasingly expanded in the abiding knowledge that, I would not be abandoned by "The Heaven Seven's Love", and their loving purpose and guidance for my life. I could feel their comforting presence during every step of my lifetime journey back to my earth body, and the life I had almost totally forgotten. Ultimately one day, I would be guided by them personally, and rejoin them on my return, back to my Heavenly Home. This would now be a newly perceived life, with a clearly defined purpose, on a substantive earthly mission. Although I did not completely comprehend or realize it at the time, I would fully recognize that, I would never be alone, in accomplishing my lifetime's true, **"Soul, Role, Goals..."**

Contemplation #05:
*"Everything began to glow from within,
more intensely in hue...
Till only a Translucent Golden Radiance,
permeated my view..."*

Chapter Six

Walking the Line between Here and the Hereafter

(The NDE translation of Michael William AngelOh)

I became more acutely aware of my seemingly lifeless body, now floating effortlessly and facing upwards, as I witnessed a golden cord of Light appear before me. This cord appeared to be a **conduit for Light** proceeding out from within the center of my corporeal chest and Heart area. I could sense that this golden cord of Light, began pouring a fluid sparkling golden Light like substance, directly into my physical body. This link of Light appeared much like a fetal cord, feeding my lifeless body with the revivifying Light of Life. Devoid of all life force for a time during my unforeseen Afterlife departure, my body continued to drink in this

99

luminous substance, as if it were the Living Waters of Life itself. The Life giving Light continued to reanimate the physical body which I had so happily forgotten, had ever existed. As this greatly desirable Light continued to pour itself into what now began to feel like a more palatable living body again, the Light continued to draw me in and ever closer to the body I have since referred to as; "**My earth suit**". I was filled with a great wonderment at all that was now occurring within me. Not quite as yet acclimated, or even close to Being comfortable within that body, I continued to experience myself floating some distance away, and outside of its enclosure. With each passing moment as the shimmering Light continued to pour itself into that once lifeless body, I felt myself Being drawn ever closer into it, until I became what I would define as; "**Being absorbed into the body**". Then came a point where I was becoming fully engaged into that body and might once again, start to think of it and perhaps even refer to it, as my body. Suddenly I observed what I can only describe as a giant hand with cupping fingers, consisting of a brilliant Golden Light reach under what I now felt was that tiny structure of my physical body. Now a bit more acclimated within my body yet still lying limply and in a silent supine position, I was facing toward the top of the Ocean waters, and the deep blue Sky itself. As I remained safely cradled within the center palm of this great golden translucently lit hand, I could feel my little body Being scooped up and lifted ever higher, toward the sky and through the deep blue and salty waters, within the depths of the Ocean. I could vividly see brilliant shafts of Sunlight streaming down and through the salty waters and toward my now limited field of vision below.

My body seemed to be lit up, as the Golden Hand continued to carry me in and through the many shimmering Lights cascading themselves, around my bodies newly reanimated existence. As the elevation of my body increased, I could see through the crystal clear Ocean waters all the way up to the very surface of the Ocean's waves, crashing themselves up and above me. The Sun's radiantly piercing shafts of Light, still penetrating through the deep blue Ocean waters. It appeared as if each beam of Light was reaching down to touch, hold, and guide my way back upward and toward the surface of the rippling waters. Suddenly, much like a cork bursting out of a deeply submerged captivity, my body popped high up, and above the Ocean water's surface as I felt my lungs explode wide open with a loud, popping sound. A rush of new and fresh air rapidly filled my oxygen starved lungs. With a quick series of deep air suction exchanges, I drank in all the life giving sustenance that I once thought would have never return to me. Floating effortlessly atop the Ocean's watery surface, my very first vision was of the radiant Sun, beaming it's bright and brilliant golden Light so strongly, from high in the sky above.

I could feel the Sun's Golden Light shining forth its deep penetrating warmth and life giving radiance, which lit up my body and all of its senses, **like a Christmas tree just plugged into its electrical source**. A few moments later, without remembering how I had gotten there, I found myself washed up and lying at the very edge of the seashore, with the Ocean's waves splashing up and against the anterior of my body. I was fully awake now and wide eyed, as if I were inside a suspended state of shier and awe-struck disbelief. As I stood up, although I could not feel my legs or feet, I began walking, more like floating, or gliding along, the sandy beach surface and onto the wooden stairway structure leading up to the Beach Boardwalk itself. As if just remotely interested in all that was happening, I headed straight down the center of the strolling crowds of people with the noisy carnival rides, along the center alleyway of the busy Boardwalk. I moved gracefully forward as if floating on a cloud. I was not aware of controlling my own bodies movements or direction, yet something was carrying my physical form along and forward. I surrendered thoughts of having any personal control over what was happening to me, and simply submitted myself to the feeling that I was no longer in charge of my bodies independent movements, functions, or ongoing experiences.

As my body glided effortlessly onward, I witnessed multiple cords of Light tied into and through the tops of the heads, and around the mouths and nostrils of every person, animal, and living creature, I encountered along my way. These **brilliantly translucent strings of Light** seemed to be **tied directly into the breath** of all living things, as each of them moved along conducting what they might have thought, were their individual and personalized lives. It appeared as if all lifeforms here were like puppets on Light strings, Being directed by their every breath of animating life-force. The golden Light strings consisted of what appeared to be a kind of sparkling glowing phosphorous substance which provided the life current necessary, to animate and guide each formed Entity, on its individual pathway through life. All life itself then, seem to be initiated from within each breath's own guiding Light flowing in rhythmic successions, one upon the other. It all appeared to look much like some **grand parade of Living Dolls** animated, directed and maneuvered by; "**The Sun's own, Solar Strings of Light**", all Being projected from high above. Everything seemed to be moving along consciously or unconsciously, controlled by the various intensities of Golden Light passing in and through, each life forms breathing mechanisms. It was as if each living entity lived, moved, and had their Beings relegated, to their own individual and personal breath filled, Solar and Life force connection. The Light's current personalizing each life through its channeled Light force frequencies. Not a single person, animal or even Seagull, seem to notice my presence as I glided forward and on by, each and every lifeform. It was as if I were now completely invisible, to all in existence that travelled on the paths of their individual dramas, all about me. This was the first time I had ever felt totally translucent, to the vision or awareness of the people around me. I had never before seen such strings of Golden Light, directing life forms along the respective journeys of their present and unfolding lifetimes.

As I continued to freely observe the boardwalks carnival atmosphere without any effort, I shall never forget the vision of the Sun's transmission of Light Strings, connected through the breathing mechanisms, of all perceived and living creatures. Now it was revealed to me that the "Sun It Self" was in control of all earth life, with breathing as its channel or energy conduit. The Sun's Light, in charge of all life's activities and functional capabilities for every life's very Being, and existence in this world. This vision and revelation would remain deeply embedded in my waking state subconscious and greatly affect all of my future lifetime perceptions. The enduring realization was that the very life force animating all life forms in all of creation from day to day, was coming directly from the Sun, the source of all Light in our world and the greater Universe, in which it exists. The sole and ultimate source of Light, sustaining all life everywhere then, was the "Sun It Self". The Sun has been at the center of my thoughts and daily contemplations each and every day, ever since. I have conceived of an exemplary description of this otherwise meta-physical vision of Solar connected life force, and its vivifying life energy transmission. If you can envision electricity, which runs our everyday technology, electronics, and appliances, you know that without power or electricity these various daily wonders, would cease to function altogether. The Sun's Light then, is like the electricity which powers so many functional tools that we use in our everyday lives. Unplugging from the Solar or Sun's Light then, would be much like unplugging tools or appliances from electricity, which would cause all such things to immediately, stop operating. Our breathing then is comparable to these power cords, transmitting their channeled electricity directly to the appliances and electronics, we use daily. This analogy is direct and should be quite simple to understand. The Sun's Light is life's electricity, and the breathing represents the power cords that direct its luminous energy as life giving electricity, to the appliances representing all living forms, and their operational functions in life. When the current of electricity is not strong enough, the appliance will not operate. When the power cord of breathing is not plugged in properly, the appliances of life do not work or may become short circuited. In this meta-physical metaphor the **"Current of Electricity"**, is **"Sunlight"**. The **"Power Cord"**, is the **"Breathing"**. The **"Appliances"**, are either the **"Body"**, or anything that needs life force and energy current to operate. When electricity stops running, then appliances don't operate, and when the Sun's Light stops Being conducted through the breathing, then in this world, that would be known, as death.

As my physical body continued to be reanimated into action, by these Solar cords of infilling life giving and golden Light, I continued to float along while moving forward upon my feet and legs which I still could not feel. I remained totally unaware of the passage of time which had elapsed as if I were living in a lifetime, that only some ancient future Entity had known, some long time ago. As it turns out, what I had both perceived and experienced to be many hours or even days of time passage during my NDE, may have actually ended up taking only some unknown minutes, of real earth time. I fully realized I was having little or no control over all unfolding events and found myself at the end of my Boardwalk journey, with my body sitting next to one of the large wooden beach pylons. There my body was placed down along a large pillar of wood jutting out beyond the sand, some one-hundred feet or so in distance, from where I saw my family still seated on the beach, enjoying their picnic luncheons. They were all together happily munching away on sandwiches on that familiar and sandy Seashore. As I watched them all I saw some wavering formation, which looked much like the sight of a mirage one might see in the Summertime heat, hovering high upon the distant sands. For just that moment then, it appeared that all I was now viewing was as if it were all a fading mirage and this sensory existence were truly, only an illusion of perception. How very detached I then felt from this projected reality of my re-entry into the material world. I seem to still be separated from my body and its sensory units, as I observed my head glancing downward and into the palm of my hand. I now observed some multi-colored projection of Light like a brightly lit three-dimensional hologram of the entire Boardwalk, including all of its rides, the Roller Coaster and Ferris Wheel.

I was able to observe both children and adults playing games and riding rides, all animated and shrunk down in size as they unfolded themselves within the very palm, of my open hand. Before this vision had faded and would ultimately vanish all together, I recall thinking that all of life's existence, including everyone's individually perceived mellow dramas and lifetime stories, were unfolding themselves through the Sun's Light and Life force, from day to day. I wondered how many of them realized the influence of the Sun's Light manifesting in their own lives, through the breath that they each consumed wittingly, or unwittingly. All of this life then, appeared to be very much like a carnival of rides I was now viewing openly, in the center of my hand. Everything I was given to observe was Being unfolded and projecting from the breath's conduction, in the "Sun's Glowing Strings" of "Life Giving Light". This vision and the association with the Life Living Light, gave me the direct impression that each life form had already chosen their own pre-selected carnival ride to ride, and that this choice would determine the experience and outcome of existence, during their lifetimes. Each life taking its own journey towards an ultimate purpose and its own pre-selected; **"Reason for Being"**. This meta-physical perception of existence, in the carnival ride each living Entity had chosen to take, has never left my consciousness or present daily awareness in living life, ever since.

At such a time, I had noticed I was again in a fully upright and stationary position moving forward toward my family, who were all still seated and now playing together, making figures and castles in the sand. As I was still a few feet away, my Mother asked in an urgent tone of voice; *"Michael, where have you been..?"* As if I were still not quite connected to my body and its mouth that was now Being prompted to operate, I heard my own voice reply, as if from some distance away say; *"I was walking on the Boardwalk..."* Just as if nothing had ever happened, I watched as my Mother then responded; *"You should have said something. We were worried about you..!"* I apologized sincerely for my temporal absence, and observed myself again as if from a distance far away. I popped open a soda and my Mom handed me one of her homemade tuna fish sandwiches from the cooler. I bit into the corner of the bread and sandwich, but could taste nothing. The entire motion of eating the sandwich seemed totally empty and tasteless to me. It was as if I were nibbling on some foreign object like cardboard, in an unnatural act of self-created pretentions, so as not to raise any suspicions as to my current state of, out of body awareness. I was then actually pretending to eat and drink, so as not to draw anyone's attention to my possible strange behavior. Yes, it felt quite odd at the time, as I had not as of yet been able to incorporate any of my behavior patterns, into my newly altered state of self-perception and reconfigured identity. All things seem to carry on as normal however, and shortly thereafter our family packed up and began making the drive back home to San Jose but I knew, and I seemed to be the only one who ever knew, from this point on, that the Michael who arrived at the beach with his family that Sunday, was not, nor would ever be, the same Michael, who left the beach for home, that day...

Contemplation #06:
*"Then as I approached some entrance,
beckoning from Heaven...
My Guardian Angels appeared before me,
and then there were Seven..."*

Chapter Seven

My Afterlife Aftermath

It's now been some fifty years since my NDE, and although until now the full story of my drowning episode has never truly been shared with anyone, the aftermath of this half century old experience has changed my perception of myself, and my purpose for existence in this life. The point of reference I now have in how I look at others travelling through their own conscious and unconscious personal journeys, has become much more one of understanding and compassion. I still; **"Hold the Vision"**, and **"Keep the Faith"**, in all I have been given to know regarding our Sun shining so high above, with its Golden Light Inhabitants living together as a Heaven centered and indwelling; **Celestial**

Civilization, within the Heart of the "**Sun It Self**". I will forever remember above all else of my NDE journey, and knowing what it is like to experience your last day on earth, and finally **after thinking your life has ended**, awakening to the ultimate reality **that a new life in your Heavenly Home has just begun**, if you're in line with Divine Will and the Divine Plan, that is. Now although not as bright and apparent as it once was, I still see the life forms here on earth, as ever radiant Light Beings operating through and from within the source and Being sustained directly, from the "**Sun's Light of Life**", shining upon us all. Also that this Light from the Sun resides inside every life form and that "**It's Presence**", establishes the foundation for all primal existence not only on earth, but throughout our entire Universe and the many other Universes or Mansions, that we as the human race may not recognize, are in existence today.

I now have some well-defined future insights, on the direction of my Soul's own personal journey in this earthly life. I fully recognize that each and every day presents me with; "**Love Lessons**", during my attendance in; "**The Earth School of Loving**", in this human existence. Another way I have heard it said would be; "**That we are Spiritual Beings having a human experience**". I noticed I have also ever since my NDE most commonly referred to my existence on earth as; "**My so called life...**" Why..? Because there is no "**My**". We have never possessed Life. It has been given to us by the Creators of Life, and if we take care of it properly, following the Creators or Owners Operational Manual, then we run with Divine Will and are rewarded accordingly. Some examples of the inner transformations I have also embraced would include, Being more considerate and caring of the Thoughts and Feelings that others may wish or need, to express. This is the case especially for those who seem more conspicuously in serious consideration of the basic needs in this life such as; food, shelter, and of course a generous level of respect. I recognize now that every life form deserves a high level of regard, just for taking a **"Birth on earth"**, and maintaining its existence here. Also I find I am much more compassionate and sensitive to those who may display loneliness or feel alienated, where perhaps an encouraging word or a simple smile of unconditional care from me, might make or break their experience in life, on any given day.

Having been raised in a strict Irish Italian and highly moral Roman Catholic home, I had always looked forward to going to Mass each and every Sunday, due to a deep desire to hear the Bible's scriptural readings and teachings. These readings called; **"The Word of God"**, I had always felt an abiding comfort from upon hearing. I can recall going to Church from early childhood and feeling a simple inner joy in looking at and through, the **glorious stained glass windows** of the **"Sacred Scenes"**, and **"Heavenly Characters"** displayed there. In the Catholic Church we attended as a family each and every Sunday morning, I had always been entranced by these luminous stained glass windows, paintings, and the sculptures present, within the Church. I seem to have a particular fixation on the most radiant colored Lights, I would see shining through the many stained glass windows which appeared before me, as early as at five years of age. The visions of resplendent Light that flowed so brilliantly through, in shimmering and bright halos of color, were always a dominant focus of my attention during Mass services. I can remember initially observing these **"Sacred Visions"**, just around the time of my first Church visit which was documented around my; **"First Holy Communion"**.

Although I had always been secretly attracted to stained glass windows, I would continue to see many of them and the sacred images they displayed, move as if they were Being animated and coming alive before me. I could always count on receiving an experience of great comfort, as I focused on the Sacred Personages and scenes they depicted. This caused me to have a deeper desire to go to Churches where I could find and get closer to the stained glass windows and particularly those depicting; **"The Lord, Jesus Christ"**, and members of; **"The Holy Family"**. If a Church didn't have stained glass windows, I would quietly move on to another Church, seeking the sacred glass. I could normally count on the Catholic Churches to have the most beautiful stained glass windows of all. My entrancement with stained glass has only grown deeper over the years, and become much more of a visionary experience for me, each and every time I'm in close proximity to them. Being of the Roman Catholic faith has created what became a need to go to Mass more regularly, and for many years I began attending Mass services early each and every morning. During these years, I sought out Church services which presented the liturgy in Latin, as I had taken two years of the Latin language at my father's insistence in High School. He called Latin the root of all languages, but for me it became the root to an ancient tongue, which provided me with visions of Monks and Monasteries, during a more ancient time. This represented a quiet and secluded world I increasingly craved to live in, from day to day. Listening to these Masses in Latin, became a language for my own transcendental journeys of mind and Heart. Such things only increasing my desire to become ever closer to God, and live by their "Divine Laws for Life".

I can recall on numerous occasions while watching the stained glass window figures, that when the Sun's Light was shining through their translucent glass, their mosaic forms would begin to appear as if in motion, especially around the face and eyes of each various and revered, "Holy Figure". A manifestation of their luminous realities projected themselves before me, in and through the numerous and color filled pieces of the translucent and sacred glass. I became transfixed in my observations of these icons, especially toward those of the Holy Family windows, and statues positioned inside the sacred spaces of the Church. At times I had noticed they seem to be **opening and closing their eyes**, staring directly at me. The first time this occurred I had looked at my family and the other parishioners as if wanting to say; **"Did you see that..?"** Of course no one around me had the surprised look, I must've had on my face as I thought I was either hallucinating, or having a Divine visitation that was meant for me alone. I finally decided I was not hallucinating, and a feeling of Being transformed through this experience of witnessing their; **"Sacred and Living Presence"**, caused me to believe that Church was the very best place to be, on all the earth. As this animated relationship with **"Jesus Christ"**, **"The Holy Mother Mary"**, **"The Saints and Apostles"**, carried on throughout my early formative years, I became the first one dressed and ready to go to Mass, each and every Sunday morning.

Then perhaps during my later teen years, when I became more socially engaged through Music and High School interactions, my visions and relationships with the Sacred Figures began to subside. I still very much looked forward to going to Church, but the thrill of these Divine encounters had concluded altogether by the time I was seventeen years of age. It has been just in more recent years while attending **St. Michael's Church**, *yes that's really the name of the Church*, that I have begun to see the Sacred images through the brightly colored pieces of glass reappear and begin to move me, once again. My experience of silent communications through the stained glass windows with the Holy Family, brought to life by the movement of the Sun's Light, becomes even more real to me, than the people who are attending Mass and sitting in the pews of the Church all around me. My childhood interaction with; **"The Transcendental Jesus Christ"**, was actually what caused me to receive him, in a most direct and natural way as my; **"Personal Lord, and Redeemer"**, at the age of twelve years old. I can honestly say that these sacred relationships with the Light, became even more meaningful to me after my NDE. Besides recording; **"Devotional and Inspirational Music"** in my **"Home Recording Studio"**, the Sacred Time I set aside to speak with the Holy Family, is the most meaningful, engaging and transformative minutes of my days, weeks, months and years, that I hope and pray, will never end.

After my NDE I became much more interested, some might say transfixed, by the vision of the Sacred Heart and the sacraments of Holy Communion and my Baptism in water, now Being consummated through the brilliance of Sunlight, vivifying the Sacred images of the Holy Family, and their Saints. Two words which might have summed up this period of time now gone by in my life's journey would be; **"Surrender and Remember"**. "Surrender", because that's what it took for me to let go of my own self-created personal struggle to breathe and survive while drowning under the

114

Ocean on; "**0828**". That surrender extended itself over from the Ocean's waters onto the mellow-dramas of life playing themselves out, upon the earth itself. On that day while I was dying and exiting from a world of characters and personal intentions I had known, I was able to acknowledge and accept a much larger, more spacious and Heavenly World view of a Celestial reality and its living Light Beings, that transcended any reality of an existence, that this earth world had to offer. And then "**Remember**", because when in my "**Spiritually Ascended State**", I realized everything I observed and experienced, seemed to be extraordinarily familiar to me, as if I were remembering something I had already seen and experienced previously and long ago, yet had forgotten over the conspiracy of lifetime events captivating, the temporal circumstances and situations now long ago, already forgotten and gone by.

As I grew up throughout the subsequent years with my loving brothers; **Denny, Patrick, Rico,** and my beloved sisters; **Vivianna,** and **Jeanette,** we were sternly guided by my **father; George William,** and the dedicated care of our ever loving **Mother; Olga Iris,** also well known to our friends and family members as; **"Mamma Olga"**. During that time in my life living at home with family, I maintained a total state of silence regarding my NDE journey. All those many years, totally unable to speak a single word of it with family members or personal friends. As a matter of fact, I found that I was unable to speak to anyone else about my NDE save my Personal Diary, and of course my Holy Family Friends, who visited me through the stained glass windows. I just could never quite fathom how I could broach the subject of my death and Heavenly World visitation with anyone, without spelling out all the many details of my paranormal experiences. And so I kept everything quiet, held deeply within and secretly hidden from everyone, until I was in my later twenties and then only with a few of my closest primary relationships. Yes, I tried my best to look and function normally, so as not to let on that something I knew, most everyone else might consider to be very strange, had happened to me. It didn't make things any easier when I would continue to experience numerous what are known as; **"OBE's"**, or **"Out of the Body Experiences"**.

These OBE's continued to occur to me throughout my childhood, adolescence, and then well into my adult years. The OBE's occurred primarily during the early morning hours usually between two and four am each morning. These OBE's might have seemed like dreams of a kind, but they would involve more vivid experiences during which I became able to observe my body sleeping in my bed, just below me. Without any effort or pre-meditation, I would observe my own physical body in its sleep position from up above, with my observation point Being some six to eight feet, in an elevated height. Many such times I would hear the same question which had formed within my mind during my NDE so many years earlier when I had asked; *"How am I able, to see my body..?"* I would once again hear that nonverbal voice whispering, like an echo from within the caverns of my mind say; *"Not with those eyes, do you see..."* I always remembered then Being introduced to another body, with another set of eyes, along with other sensory units, which we as humans rarely seem to be aware of and are much less able to directly experience. For the most part, most folks seem to remain totally unaware of what I have ever since referred to as; **"The Soul Body"**, during the course of their entire earthly lives. I had seen this other body was fashioned from a golden white and translucent Light and of course, as the years went by I became totally comfortable in continuing to think of it as my; **"Soul Body",** and the movement of it as; **"Soul Travel"**.

For some time, I decided I'd simply write off my OBE's, as some far out reoccurring dream of my Soul, leaving my dormant physical body behind, in my bed positioned just below me. I found myself travelling about the house, and then leaving the house, usually through a skylight window or through the top of the ceiling. I would rise above the roof of my home, above the trees, and above other homes that appeared just below me, to the place I knew was my local neighborhood. These journeys of my Soul would often lead to an arrival at a body of water, located close by to wherever I happened to be living at the time. I had always desired and eventually arranged, to live in close proximity to either the Ocean, a reservoir, or a Lake front location. My Soul Travel destinations would usually lead me back to one of these bodies of water, but more often than not, I would be taken back to the Ocean and Beach, where I had my original NDE encounter, in Santa Cruz California. The **"Soul Traveling Journeys"** I went on, occasionally occurred a little closer to home where I had lived for a time in; Los Gatos California, nearby a serene body of water known as; **"Lake Vasona"**. I would linger about such a place and feel as if I were floating just over and above the surface of the water for what seemed like hours at a time. For many years after my NDE, especially during my **"Translation Anniversary Month of August"**, I would wake up in my physical body, and my bed sheets would be soaking wet, as if I had just gotten out of the Ocean and plopped down into the bed, without ever drying off. During this same month of August, I would have many dreams and flashbacks of my NDE, detailing moments I had ever since forgotten during the subsequent years. These recollections might have been mostly forgotten in time, if they were not recorded within the pages of my; **"Personal Daily Diary"**.

It was at the age of nineteen, that I reached a contentious critical point with my father, and his personally enforced house rules. It had been a time during the late 1960's, after many years of playing percussion instruments, first beating on pots and pans as a child at home, then progressing to various types of drums and bells once I had entered my School years. I had become a section leader at my Elementary and High School located in Cupertino California. I excelled at performing on many different percussion instruments and became the primary state drummer in our High School's Marching Band. I was able to perform at many School sporting events. I played key roles in our School's Orchestra and Jazz Bands. I had started a Rock Band, and was auditioning various Musicians to make up what I hoped would be a successful Musical group. The goal was to make a little money by performing for dance concerts at our High School. I set some pretty high standards in recruiting the Musicians I was considering. I was able to source some very good ones at the local Moyer Brothers Music store, located just a few miles away from where I had been living at our Parent's Home, in San Jose California. After auditioning some half dozen different Musicians, I finally was able to select the ones I felt were the most talented and could perform in a successful Music venue together. This group of Musicians later became Internationally well known as a Top-40 Band, whose name I will only disclose by the letters; **"DB"**. Our Music Concerts brought me even more notoriety than I had ever imagined, or wanted. I recall the Band performing for my High School's dance concert and during the break, having girls I didn't know and had never even met, want to share their bodies with me. One night, I had offers from three different girls who wanted me to visit them for intimate relations at their homes, after the show.

Of course I still held onto all of my Catholic morals, and never did except any of those invitations, but I was still blown away at how easy these people were willing to give away their intimacy. I became quite popular as a result of my Rock Music status at my High School and because I couldn't escape my own internal nature, I spent my time avoiding the classmates, who wanted to hang out with me. I never liked Being popular or sought after. My desire had always been to **become invisible, once again**. Then we had set up a major gig at a place called; **"The Chateau Liberte"** located, in the Santa Cruz Mountains. There would be hundreds of folks in attendance and we would all make more money than we had ever been able to score before. On the day of the concert we arrived just before play time and I noticed, there were about a dozen Hell's Angel members in attendance, wandering about the grounds before the show. That didn't appeal to me too much because I immediately felt, that could mean trouble. Folks were smoking marijuana straight out in the open, and our lead guitarist was already shooting up behind the stage. He was with what appeared to be both a black and a white hooker and inviting me to join him. I made some kind of lame excuse not to participate, like I had to tune-up my drums or something like that. As it all turned out, I managed to avoid most of the insanity and we had a successful show and all got to make it back home, safely. I was already wondering if this was the kind of Music life I had envisioned for myself. Fortunately, the Bass Player didn't do drugs either, and I was able to spend most of my free time between our gigs with him.

Then came the day of reckoning, when my father became convinced after a Band jamming practice one Saturday afternoon in our Family House garage, that my new Musician friends were drug addicts, and the kind of people he liked to call; **"Hippies"**. These individuals were going to seriously be a bad influence on me, and perhaps my brothers as well. It all culminated in his proclaiming an ultimatum later that Saturday, which was either to quit the Band, or leave and move out of the house altogether. Having never known another Home, or how I would create an alternative living situation, I caved, and quit the Band. My father seemed quite pleased and reminded me as he had so many times before, that there was no money in Music and that playing Music should be considered only as a hobby, and not as a livelihood. What a paradox it became then, and how none of us could have ever known, that I would make more money in Music than either of us could have ever imagined, for over twenty-five years in the Music business, later in my life. Two weeks later the Bass player for the Band I had assembled drove up in front of our house, in his new fully decked out, tuck and rolled interior, beautiful black Van with flashing mag wheels. I watched him pull up into our homes driveway and so walked out to meet him. I asked him where he got the new Van, to which he responded; **"We just signed a contract for a Music Album release with Warner Brothers Music..."** I asked; **"You mean you got a contract with the recording I played drums on, then you guys submitted it to Warner Brothers..?"** **"Yep..."** he said. Just at that time my father strolled out to see what was happening, and I told him what the Bass Player had just told me. The Bass Player then added he had just received an advance payment of some $30,000 which he used to purchase his new and deluxe vehicle. My Heart sunk at this sudden occurrence and I became deeply disturbed. I felt totally betrayed by my father and my previous decision to quit the Band. I suddenly spurted out the words to my father; **"I thought you said, there wasn't any money in Music..?"** I saw a puzzling look I had never before seen on my father's face as he stated; **"That's just one in a million Michael. Just one in a million..."** Then in an angered tone of voice I replied; **"Yah, I was that one in a million..."** then I said, **"See yah..."** to the Bass Player, and stormed off to my bedroom.

Later that same Saturday I confronted my father, with all the hostility I had now developed, within my massively disappointed state of consciousness. The abrasive discussion ended up with me shoving my father, into the Kitchen room wall. He struck it hard and for the first time I realized, I was stronger than my father. I would no longer have to submit to his tyranny. I would never accept his constrictive rules to confine my life or my chosen desired lifetime activities ever again. Within some twenty-four-hours I had quite suddenly moved out of my Parents home and **into a Christian Yoga Temple**, also located in San Jose California. I share this story only because it led to a radical departure from the path I was travelling on, and into another lifetime journey, which I would have never recognized or accepted, if it were not for leaving the Rock scene with its drug inductions and highly questionable morals. I officially began my Spiritual path as many have done, as a direct result of enduring a broken Heart and the feeling of betrayal, by one I had Loved. As I learned about Yoga, Meditation, and Spiritual evolvement, I

121

discovered some time later by meeting the lead guitarist of the Band I had originally assembled, that they were on a grueling schedule of touring performance dates, to promote their new Music Album release. This talented although ego-centered guitarist, was now suffering from some massive intestinal ulcerations which prevented him from performing, and into a liquid diet to heal all the internal intestinal damage he was suffering from. Immediately after this meeting, I recall thinking of my father, and silently thanking him for what up till that point, was a very unpleasant memory he had been such an integral part of co-creating. In essence I finally forgave my father, and continued to embrace my new Spiritual path in large part, thanks to him.

Although I had never surrendered my Catholic faith, I found myself moving into this **"Christian Yoga Spiritual Community"**, that taught both the Hindu Philosophy of Yoga and Meditation blended with; **"Greek Orthodox Christianity"**. This move represented the opening of an entirely new chapter in my life. My new living environment brought some significant changes to my attitude and appearance including, learning how to quiet my mind through the physical; **"Stretching Postures of Yoga"**, coupled with the Mind focusing exercises practiced through the **"Art, of Meditation"**. I was also very well pleased to discover that; **"Breath Control exercises called, Pranayama"**, were an integral part of the Yoga Training program I was undertaking. It wasn't long before my breathing became deeper, more rhythmic, and much slower than ever before. All of this training along with the continued growth of my long flowing and wavy hair, that now extended down to my buttocks, gradually changed the way I felt and definitely changed the way I looked. Within just a few months at the Yoga Temple, I became much more mentally focused, with a steady gaze developed through my many hours of daily stretching postures and Meditation practice. I integrated my newly discovered lifestyle in this **Yoga Community**, also called an **Ashram** meaning; **"Spiritual Hermitage"** or **"Temple"** in the Indian Sanskrit language. Within a six-month period of training and intense study, I was now teaching Beginner's Yoga and Meditation classes, wearing custom and embroidered Yoga apparel, often hand made for me by my Yoga students. My new studies in Yoga and Hindu Mysticism brought a great concern to my immediate family and in particular to my beloved Parents, who primarily on the part of my father, had accused me of losing my Catholic faith and leaving my Christian religion. This significant lifestyle change occurred to me during the early 1970's, and for a time I could be seen sporting a 350-Honda motorcycle along the California freeways, with my long wavy hair trailing behind me like some sort of comet tail. These inner and outer transformations really began in earnest during the Summer of 1971, as my appearance and demeanor aligned themselves with my evolving practice from beginning to more advanced Yoga postures, coupled with daily two-hour long Meditation periods. By the end of my first year of Spiritual Temple studies, I discovered that I began wearing ever brighter and more custom handmade clothing and wore some twelve rings, and that was just on my right hand.

I lived, worked, and taught, at the Yoga Community for nearly two years, which was very strict about leaving the Temple to engage in any sort of outside activity. Such interaction with the outside world was not considered to be in accordance with Temple work and progress on the

Spiritual path. Our rather intense and modest Community of Temple students was assigned a daily work schedule which included teaching Yoga classes, and working at the Temple's Health Food Store located on 4th Street in downtown San Jose. The store was always busy due to its location Being one block in proximity to San Jose State University. The only exception for leaving Temple grounds and our twelve-hour daily work schedule was if we were granted permission to leave, and such a "leave of absence" only after the first year of Temple residency. After this first year, we were allowed to petition our instructor also known as; **"The Guru"** meaning; **"Spiritual Teacher"**. Once a written petition was submitted and approved, a four hour leave of absence could be granted to share in the Temple's pre-authorized and specific holidays of; **Easter, Thanksgiving, and Christmas,** and then only with immediate family members. This could be accomplished on a day after morning services and Temple duties were completed. I recall such a Holiday, riding up on my motorcycle to our family gathering place for a full course Italian dinner with my family in the early afternoon on; **Thanksgiving Day, 1972.** As I pulled up to my Grandparent's home located in Santa Clara California, and walked up to the front door, I could hear the usual gregarious conversations and laughter Being shared among my family members seated inside.

As I knocked on the door, a sudden and deafening silence fell over the sounds of frivolity and as the front door slowly opened, there appearing directly in front of me was my beloved Grandmother, whom we as family affectionately called; **"Nonna"**, meaning **"Grandmother in Italian"**. I embraced her as I had always done, and with her arms still wrapped around me she whispered quietly into my left ear;

"We pray, that you come back to us Michael..." I could feel her pain at her perceived loss of perhaps what she thought of as, the losing of my Soul. Now I would feel even more strongly than ever before that I might be considered primarily by the senior members of our family, to be the proverbial **"Black Sheep"** in the family. My Mother was the next in line to greet me at the door and she expressed nearly the same sentiments as my Grandmother had shared in her whispers, just a few moments earlier when she spoke the words; *"We are praying for you Michael..."* I then took my assigned seat at the family dinner table as everyone else remained silent around me for what felt like an uncomfortable period of time.

Then I said something like; *"Well, what are we having for dinner..?"* My sister Vivianna was the first to respond outlining the multiple courses of homemade exquisitries, on the elaborate menu consisting of the many Italian dishes that we normally celebrated with every holiday. My younger sister Jeanette was next to join in on the conversation talking about Nonna's wonderful homemade Italian bread buns. They had just been baked and rested lightly steaming in a basket, warmly and fragrantly just in front of us on the dinner table, wondering who would be the first to reach for their toasty goodness. It wasn't long before my three brothers known at that time as; Dennis, Patrick, and Richard joined in on the conversation as my father sat stoically, at the head of the table for a few unengaging minutes then suddenly chimed in saying; *"You look like you're in some kind of a trance..."* Everything went quite once again, as I sat very still within the uncomfortable silence that dropped upon me. I assured my father that I was not in any kind of trance state, but rather had been practicing Meditation, a

125

contemplative exercise to make still and quiet, my mind. I further explained that what he might have perceived as a trance state, was actually my greatly increased ability to focus and direct my mind's attention, into a single pointed state of consciousness. Surprisingly my Mother then commented that she had heard of Meditation and might be interested in taking one of my classes, to learn more about the subject. My father quickly followed up to my Mother's comment saying; *"We have our own Meditation..."* referring to their prayer time. His comment effectively ended the subject and my Mother's interest and potential involvement in enrolling for one of my classes held at a nearby College.

I knew in short order my father then believed, I was involved in some kind of occult group and I could now officially be considered; a lost Soul. This was only confirmed in my father's mind after he had learned I had surrendered my given birth name and had received the new Spiritual name; **"OmSurya"**, which then evolved to the name; **"SunSurya"**. I had been given this new name by **Ram Dass**, one of my Spiritual teachers during the 1970's who told me the name meant; **"Keeper of the Rainbow, in the Sun of God..."** My father later found out that Ram Dass had taken the hallucinogenic drug LSD, and so was now to be considered a druggie, a hippie, and therefore a negative and occult influence on my life. What was particularly memorable about the whole experience was that toward the end of my visit, I became convinced that all of my brothers and sisters, and even my Parents and Grandparents sensed, that I wasn't as evil or lost, as they might've originally thought me to be upon my arrival for the Holiday meal that Thanksgiving Day. This was primarily confirmed on my departure when I received a hug from each and every family member, with the noticeable exception of my father. Nearing the front door to make my exit, I received some of the same comments I had originally been given by my Mother and Grandmother regarding their praying for me. This time however their hugs seemed much warmer and more authentic than I had received when I had first presented myself before them. My beloved family and our Thanksgiving dinner was most memorable on this loving family Holiday. I was all of twenty years of age, at that time.

Toward the end of my second year at the Yoga Temple, I had studied World Religions along with Christian Mysticism and Greek Orthodox Christianity. As my life's Spiritual journey continued to unfold itself and the years rolled by, I became increasingly interested in the Paranormal Metaphysical disciplines and Spiritual Healing Arts, which would evolve themselves into my teaching a weekly curriculum of some twenty-four classes in Yoga, Meditation, Acupressure Massage and Color Healing all held at various Colleges, the YMCA's, and extended Adult Instructional Community Centers. These days unfolded during the early 1970's when the Beatles Music group was flying off to India meeting with the Guru; **"Maharishi Mahesh Yogi"**, and learning his Meditation technique known as; **"Transcendental Meditation"**, or simply; **"TM"**. As a result of their International publicity, Yoga and Meditation became very popular in the US, with the Beatles Eastern engagements and especially **George Harrison's** involvement, within the "**Hare Krishna Movement**".

It wasn't long before I was teaching to groups of people registered for my Yoga and Meditation classes, exceeding one hundred students in number, Being held at San Jose

State University, San Jose City College, and throughout San Jose and the Greater Bay Area of California. During this time, I became the Author of four local best-selling Books which were sold to all of my own students in some twenty plus classes that I taught each week. My Books were also picked up by a large Bookstore chain with locations throughout the West Coast of the United States. It was the first time I began receiving royalty checks in the mail from Bookstore sales, for a few thousand dollars a week for doing nothing except to observe the numbers, which were posted on each check, totaling my weekly Bookstore sales. At most of the locations I was instructing at, I had teaching contracts garnering between sixty to seventy-five percent of the total registration fees which were paid by the registering students for each class. This resulted in my earning hundreds of dollars an hour for teaching an average of four, one hour classes a day, times the six days I taught each week. This was unbelievable stuff as I had never earned this quantity of money before and to me, it all seemed almost as paranormal in scope in the material world, as my now expanded perception initiated through my NDE, had been so many years earlier, in the Spiritual World. Of course life was good both Spiritually and materially, and I easily obtained whatever it was I thought I needed, and gave most of the rest of the money away to the many needy Soul's I had met along my journey.

What does all this have to do with my NDE..? Well I wouldn't have had any of these wonderful Life changing experiences had my NDE gone, the other way home. More importantly my NDE opened the door for me to walk the Spiritual path here on earth for an additional fifty plus years thus far, so I could get back to my Heavenly Home one day, with so many more beautiful memories than I could have ever had otherwise. I mentioned just a few of the most transformative stories that my NDE inspired and made possible. I truly do believe that my drowning death caused me to experience a separate reality that then directly led me to be attracted to transcendental people, places, and things in my life. Although during my childhood NDE it had seemed that I had traveled so many Light years away from earth, into the Light planet we call the Sun, I have subsequently been told by "My Heaven Seven Guardians", that these Heavenly realms actually exist in a separate reality or a parallel Universe, which dwells side by side with all of its Heavenly inhabitants, adjacent to the very different reality we seem to be experiencing in this human life, here on the earth. This greatly helped me to understand the meaning of the Biblical passage;

"Neither shall they say, Lo here! or, lo there! for behold, The Kingdom of God is within you..."
~Luke 17:21 (NIV)

I had always wondered what the words; **"The Kingdom of God is within you..."** meant. As a direct result of my NDE I now know that it means to live and hold "One's Being" in a; **"Divine State of Consciousness"**, so then the distance between us and Heaven might be well summed up in the following Scriptural passage;

"Do not conform to the pattern of this world, but be transformed by the renewing of your mind. Then you will be able to test and approve what God's will is, his good, pleasing and perfect will..."
~Romans 12:2 (NIV)

So the distance between this life in the material world of human existence, and the Heavenly realms may well exist in the distance between, who we think we are, and the; **"Renewing of our Minds"** or as **Chance' Gardener,** played by *Peter Sellers* echoes in my all-time favorite movie; **"Being There"** states; **"Life, is a state of Mind..."** or perhaps we might add; **"A state of Divine Mind..."**

I also became more extraordinarily focused on my breathing, as one of the very most important commodities for living a life upon the earth. If it were not for my NDE, I may have never realized how very vital the need to continuously develop deeper and a more regulated breath by breath control, on a daily basis truly is. This breathing in and breathing out process comes so automatically and yet can be so easily forgotten, taken for granted, and unwittingly dismissed as too ordinary or happenstance, to be of any importance. Because I have known what it was like to die for a breath, I no longer overlooked the breath's all pervasive influence over my life's sustenance, that gauges the quantity and quality of life operating within, all life forms existing upon the earth. Then to discover that breathing doesn't stop at death, was certainly one of the most surprising revelations I had ever experienced from my early childhood's NDE which continues all the way up to, the present day. This single revelation of the importance of controlling one's breathing, helped to make so many of the moments in my life which had previously seemed so strange, now make perfect sense. I became so comforted to know that of all the things that come and go in this life, the breath is always there, always with me, and one of the most direct tools to commune directly with "The Holy Spirit". Now that I have fully realized that the breath is the conductor of Light and Life, I have been able to call upon it to greatly sooth me in times of turmoil and tribulation. It is the vouchsafe channel I currently use to tune the instrument of my mind, tune to the frequency of the Heavenly realms and of course, always keep attuned to my "Heaven Seven Guardians".

If I were to share the simple formula of breathing as an affirmation with you, I would simply state it as follows:

"Breathe deeply... Live deeply...
Breathe slowly... Live slowly...
Breathe evenly... Live evenly...
Breathe harmoniously... Live harmoniously...
Breathe peacefully... Live peacefully...
Breathe in Love... Live in Love..."
Nothing more... Nothing less...

Contemplation #07:
"Now in this new world,
it was becoming increasingly clear...
That my Guardian Angels,
were always stationed, quite near..."

Chapter Eight

In Conclusion: Then, Now, & in Time Future

(The NDE translation of Michael William AngelOh)

Is there Life after Death..? For most of recorded history people from all places across our little blue planet have asked the question; **"What will happen to me when I die..?"** Most have avoided this question, but ultimately everyone will come face to face with the answer in their own time, and in their own very personal way. Many religious to non-religious beliefs range from; After death Souls will go to either a; **"Heaven or Hell"**, to the opposite side of the equation stating that; **"There is no Afterlife..."** Other insights on the cycle of rebirth and reincarnation may be pondered along the way, until each Soul finds their own true; "**Reason for Being**", and as such be more able to; "**Live a life on purpose...**" Some ancient tribal religions submit that after death, the human Soul remains upon the earth joining with other dearly departed or disembodied spirits, including those of their ancient ancestors and relatives. Many other religions teach that there is an ongoing struggle between good and evil, where Heaven ultimately reveals a bodily Resurrection for the good and saved like that demonstrated by; "**The Lord Jesus Christ**". The answers to these age old questions of life beyond the grave, seem to call for a deeper introspection and an aide in discovering the truth as is provided by developing a personal relationship with; "The Higher Power", or "The Holy Spirit", ever present within the human Soul. During the past few decades' thousands of people have reported encountering what are known as; "**Near Death Experiences**" or more simply called; "**NDE's**". NDE's are very personal experiences which through some natural or more often traumatic circumstances, cause an individual to make an expected or unannounced departure from his or her waking state awareness within the physical body. As such their consummated life force or what I have called; "**The Soul**" in this manuscript, enters into a separate realm or world of perception, with its own transcendental yet very personalized existence. Such experiences have resulted in powerful life transformations in many of the individual cases studied, including my own.

According to the latest research on NDE's, approximately fifty percent of people who survive their Near Death episodes, report an experience in which they encounter themselves to be floating above and looking down on, their own physical bodies and the immediate surroundings, in which they had died. Many of the subjects in these reported case studies appeared to have accurately described objects and events during their experiences, which they could not have seen, or known about, from the vantage point of their physical bodies recorded, dying location. A few of these studies include people who were able to accurately describe the people present and events taking place around them, even though they had been physically blind, since birth. What has been of particular interest in the reports of such NDE's, are the accurate and amazingly similar terms and details given, even though the NDE occurrences may have happened many miles or continents apart, in diverse situations, and from radically variant cultures. These details often include descriptions such as;

01-**Leaving of the body, while observing their departure from somewhere up, and above the location where they; "Gave up the Ghost..."**

02-**Traveling through a tunnel and seeing a bright and ever expanding point of Light and its approaching end, advancing toward them...**

03-**Meeting familiar Beings such as departed family and friends, who appear to be welcoming them and will often guide their way on, into the Heavenly realms...**

04-**Meeting a Spiritual Being or translucent figure of Light, who acts as a counselor and mediator, as the dearly departed travel deeper into the Afterlife...**

05-**Experiencing profound states of Peace and Unconditional Love, after which most are told that it is not their time to remain, and that they must return, to their life back on earth...**

My own Near Death Experience has taught me that death is not something to be feared, rather it is much like taking a walk through a doorway from one room, into a larger room of a separate reality in Being and consciousness. Life then is not lost or ended, but is in fact more fully lived and experienced, than ever before. I recall hearing a friend of mine whose name is **Emmanuel** say that; **"Death is like taking off, a tight shoe..."** resulting in the perception that; **"Death is totally Safe..."** Since my own NDE at fourteen-years of age, I have noticed some very interesting patterns and character developments which have evolved within my own persona, during my fifty some years of a continuation of my life on earth since that Sunday on; "0828". One of the primary transformations was, that although I had always **favored Sundays, as my very favorite day of the week,** I now longed much more deeply and prayed **that every day, would be like the sacredness I had always experienced, on Sundays.** This was a **"Day of Rest"** celebrated world-wide by billions of people. This was a day of worship, and a day of deeper thinking and Being more finely attuned to God, the Spiritual Life, and the dedicated Gifts of "The Holy Spirit". All of the most life changing blessings I have ever experienced during the course of my lifetime, have all most frequently occurred, on a Sunday. I have already mentioned the profound effect which breathing has had in my life as a direct result of my NDE. Breathing in and of itself, seems to be the moderator for many of the life changing events which would follow during the subsequent years since my childhood experience of death.

Another one of the more profound changes I had noticed after my Near Death Experience was, that I became much less talkative, and much more of a listener. I recall during

136

one of my father's childhood shouting episodes, I had been following my breathing with peak interest as a way of discharging his anger toward me, and suddenly, I couldn't hear the loudness of his voice raving at me anymore. It was as if I found the mute button, and were now able to place a silence upon the intense and unfolding drama Being displayed just before me. This new mentally initiated volume control was suddenly in effect and subsequently everything just went completely quiet, as I continued to view my father's various and somewhat contorted facial expressions, play on. It was as if I were now viewing him and the entire scene, as some kind of **"Silent Picture Movie"**. I actually had to fight not to snicker, as it all seemed so very funny at the time, just observing his muted face in its full range of motion and highfalutin outward expressions. Again I believe it was the breathing which had caused this phenomenon of mind to occur, with a refocus of the blaring sounds, now Being transformed into an absolute and highly desirable, silence. To my dear father's credit, he was able to transform his own consciousness after working so very hard and long, for so many years and suffering multiple Heart attacks, along the way. During the final decade of his life, we were able to make Peace with one another, and we even discussed meeting up in our Heavenly Home one day. That truly was one of the most meaningful conversations I ever had, with dear old dad.

During subsequent years sometime around the age of fifty, I became much more introverted as I intentionally began avoiding folks and groups of people who would assemble themselves anywhere, and everywhere. I seem to continually have this overwhelming desire to be left alone, and most usually expressed the need to be quiet or have solitary time, even when I became involved in very personal and intimate primary relationships with others. In public settings, I actually noticed I would seek out the quietest and the more isolated areas to be within, and that this would also apply to my personal engagements during all my daily activities and responsibilities as well. I recall thinking how odd it was, that I had always tried to get away from people yet ended up Being with hundreds of thousands of folks during the ten years I taught Yoga, and the thirty some years I was in the Music business. These days it seems that I have been able to come full circle, as I am able to seek a greater silence and separation from people again, not only in the Silent Sanctuaries of my mind and Heart, but in my little Hermitage for **writing Short Stories, Poems**, and **composing Inspirational Music**. Now I seem to have ever increasing flashbacks wishing to become invisible again, as I had once been as a young child, walking along the crowded Boardwalk during my NDE, in Santa Cruz California. How I had so many times greatly wished to dwell unceasingly in my Inner Sanctuary, during many of life's external maladies and challenging situations. I suppose this also led to me Being a bit claustrophobic whenever indoors or inside enclosed buildings, and the smaller tighter places of all external infrastructures. I noticed if I had to be indoors, my breathing would immediately become more shallow, and I would need to **intentionally try to breathe more deeply**, and **seek greater wide open spaces**. I still remembered what it was like to suffocate under the Ocean waters when I died, for a single breath of air.

My NDE also made it clear that, we will only know our Guardian Angels when we take the time to get to know them, and have created the circumstances in which we become ready and able, to invite them into our own personal spaces, from their Celestial Domains, into our individual and material worldly existences. This means learning to create a receptive space or what I would call a; **"Silent Soul's Sanctuary"**, in which we can open the receptive channels and capabilities of all our senses such that, we may experience each of them with a deeper focus and receptivity. If we continuously practice developing the indwelling ability to create the proper and receptive; **"Angel Invitation Atmosphere"**, we can learn how to invite the presence of our Guardian Angels, to walk into our time and space arena. When these internal receptive qualities are developed through practice, we become much more likely to recognize the presence of; **"Sacred Spaces"** and, **"Spiritual Visitations"**. One day you may also ultimately be surprised, **to meet your own Guardian Angel unannounced**, making their own Celestial appearance in your life. I invite you to make special pre-arranged time periods which I have called; **"Making Angel Time"**. I begin my own Angel invitation process by choosing a Sacred Place or Graceful Space, which I intuit may be the most inviting to the Celestial Presence of an Angel or Luminary Guide. I do this by positioning my body such that it will be still, and remain mostly motionless, in a state of rest, for a minimum of five to fifteen minutes at a time. Then I am directed to; **"Quiet my mind"**, so that it stops or minimizes the transmission of thoughts, questions, or worldly distractions.

I am able to achieve this by bringing my mind to a point of focused concentration, on a **vision toward any Light source, such as a candle flame,** or a point of Light visible and present, in any place I happen to find myself desiring to focus both mind and Heart toward; "The Holy Spirit". Once this Light point of focus has been established, I can then repeat a word or collection of words, which I have discovered my mind will be able to concentrate on and rest gently upon. My selection of words happens to be special and sacred to me, and so I can more easily collect any of the loose and unqualified mental attention which has been scattered, from wandering in the many external places it might have travelled to, during the waking state consciousness of life. Now all of that precipitous attention may be brought back and into, my concentrated focus on my "Sacred Words" and "Source of Light". My concentration on the Light, along with the circling of "Sacred Words" repeated either silently or audibly, in unceasing repetition, work together to bring all distracted attention back together into one, singularly minded place. It is the ability to collect all scattered awareness in order to enable a deeper focused consciousness, that is key to creating and expanding; "Peace of Mind" and "Making Angel Time".

Within a few minutes or however long it takes, the combination of these Light and Sound elements work together in tandem, assisting the mind to become quiet and ultimately, laser focused. This may occur in as few as a half dozen Meditation or Contemplation sessions, for the beginner. Once the mind has been re-collected, then the next stage of creating your; "Celestial Invitation" or "Angel Time", involves enhancing "Spiritual Receptivity" through the integration of a; "Quiet Mind", to an; "Open Heart". This can be accomplished by focusing the mind on the center of one's chest, directly at the location around the sternum area. This is not where one's physical beating Heart is located, but rather where what we will call one's; "Spiritual Heart", can be found. Now the fingertips of the right hand may be **Lightly placed on the central chest area** at the designated spot, and the breathing may be focused here, at this point. Each breath begins to feel as if it were Being conducted in and through, this central chest location. The slow and intentionally rhythmic breathing now begins to feel as if it was Being guided in, and out, from the center chest, such that a warmth begins to be generated in this place. Once this breathing cycle initiates, the mind will continue to collect all remaining, wandering and unqualified attention that may have once been scattered and lost. With continued practice and as mental attention is continually Being gathered and focused, one's mental concentration is then placed solely upon increasing the **"Radiance of Warmth"**, at the central chest area as described. When you can feel any trace of warmth, then this becomes your initial indication that your; **"Heart is Opening"** and your; **"Mind is Quieting"**. If an awareness toward the warmth is not yet felt, then continue the practice focusing on the central chest area from breath to breath.

Again it's the ability to focus the concentration of the mind, that eventually expands the experience of developing; **"The Spiritual Heart"** or, **"Your Sacred Heart Center"**. This practice may continue for five to fifteen minutes as the warmth from your; **"Spiritual Sacred Heart Center"**, continues to increase in its intensity. When this practice of the contemplation exercise becomes more advanced, then one's mind is continually evolving in an interior quietness and receptiveness, while one's Heart continues to generate an increasing warmth, from deep within. In time this creates a state of consciousness which not only becomes more conductive and conducive to the higher vibrations of the Celestial Spheres, but also invites the company of **your Guardian Angel, to be received.** This is the breathing, mind focusing exercise that I have found best works for any person to become more finely attuned, to the "Heavenly Realms" that are ever in existence and in what I have described is a; **"Parallel Universe or Dimension"** inside of which dwells and is immediately adjacent to, our own daily life's existence, operating here on earth. It works much like one would **tune a radio or television set** to receive the; **"Program Transmission Desired".** In this way with practice over time, one may **tune into the Celestial frequencies** and open a channel, for receiving and interacting with the Celestial or Heavenly Realms, and with one's own personal; **"Guardian Angel".**

I become more keenly aware of one or more of my Guardian Angels, when I feel a radiating warmth coming forth from my; "Spiritual Sacred Heart Center". I envision the appearance of my Sacred Heart, lit with a burning flame or golden fire, glowing from within my chest's ever growing; "Spiritual Sacred Heart". This daily practice of visualizing the Sacred Heart begins with my eyes closed, then evolves to an open vision of seeing my Sacred Heart appear, with my eyes now fully opened. This **"Sacred Heart Visualization Exercise"**, focuses one's entire mind and awareness into receiving a vision much like the Sacred Heart seen in the 18th century paintings of the; **"Sacred Heart of Jesus Christ"** or the; **"Sacred Heart of the Holy Mother Mary".** The "Sacred Heart Visualization Exercise" is then the pre-requisite for creating your; "Sacred Angel Time". Once a visualizing of "The Sacred Heart" is established, then more times than not, I have observed the body of one or more of my; **"Heaven Seven Guardian Angels"** and their Celestial forms, begin to materialize before me.

142

On one of my prior "0828 Anniversary Memorials", I had been so blessed as to see the face and even the full figured form of; "Jesus Christ" with his beloved; "Mother Mary", blazing in a vision of Glorious Light and a Holy Fire. In these rare and most transcendent moments, I could feel the fire of my Sacred Hearted Soul, Being reflected within the glorious brilliance of the Sacred Hearts glowing within the various Heavenly personages, I was then concentrating upon and envisioning. I recall one of my Guardian Angels telling me during my childhood NDE that this; **"Was a Fire, that did not burn…"** Although I know this practice of focused deep breathing and the visualization of the Sacred Heart may take weeks, months, or even years to develop, practice does truly, make perfect. This is the specified breathing and visualization exercise that has worked best from all of the many Meditation and Contemplation programs I have tried, taught, and practiced, over the many years. I hope and pray it may also work in your daily practice in developing your own; **"Sacred Heart State of Being"**. I seem to be reminded many times over during this practice of concentration on my own **"Sacred Heart State of Being"**, of some of the prayers from Sacred Biblical Scriptures which include;

> **"Create in me a clean Heart O God,**
> **and renew a right Spirit within me…"**
> *~Psalm 51:10 (KJV)*

And my other favorite;

> **"Blessed are the pure in Heart,**
> **for they shall see God…"**
> *~Matthew 5:8 (KJV)*

We must learn to cultivate this proper and receptive atmosphere, so we may become more able to invite our

Guardian Angels to visit with us, no matter where we happen to be, or what we happen to be doing. Through the daily practice of developing this; **"Sacred Heart Receptivity"**, you too will discover that your Guardian Angels are always communicating their; **"Spiritual Guidance"** and **"Heavenly Messages"**, for your life. You too can experience the mighty glory in the presence of "The Holy Spirit" and your own "Guardian Angel's" endlessly and ever enduring Kindness, Love, and robust Celestial righteousness, which they so long to share with you each and every day of your life. It was also a continuous personal revelation throughout my NDE that in truth, I fully realized that; "**God is all good... All of the time...**" So we should make every effort in our present and daily life to; "**Be all good... All of the time...**" This would include all goodness transmitted through our every; **"Thought, Word, and Deed"** each and every day. I would also like to say that during my visit to the luminous infrastructures in Heaven, although I could not identify the many human like and radiant Light Beings I had seen there by name, I intuitively knew that they were the **"Saints"**, **"Ascended Masters"**, and even the closest **"Apostles"** of; **"The Lord Jesus Christ"**, **"God the Father"**, and **"The Eternal Holy Family"**. Is it any wonder then, that more than ninety percent of those who encounter an NDE and make it through the Tunnel of Light into the Heavenly Realms, do not wish to return back to the material world, and their former lives as humans living upon the earth..? But alas, most of them are told those oh so familiar words; "**Your time, has not yet come. You must return...**"

Finally, I would say that many of the most profound transformations that have occurred to me along the journey of my life, were as a direct result of my NDE, and its profound influence on the direction and intentions, that ultimately manifested in one way or other during the course of my lifetime. The primary one Being that I no longer experienced a fear of death, or the unknown. If there was a particular challenging issue for me, it was that I would have dreams of my NDE drowning play themselves over and again, during my waking state hours. Like a flashback, although I had still drowned and ascended into the Heavenly Realms in these dreams, I was no longer faced with having to make the decision requiring that I return back, to my earth life. Somehow the arrangement with returning to assuage the heartbreak of my absence from my beloved Mother's life, was no longer an issue for me. It has in fact since my NDE become a; **"Mission Accomplished"** aspect of my life. This became conspicuously true after my beloved Mother's translation or passing from this world, to join our dear father in their Heavenly Home in the year 2014.

There was a time in that same year, that I had strongly felt that I had fulfilled many of my earthly **"Love Lessons"** and extended relationship commitments. I can recall thinking that I had now finally consummated all of the worldly duties and agreements I had made, even before the time of my birth on earth. These were a kind of pre-arrangement I had made with other Souls, who would ultimately comprise the totality of; **"My Spiritual Family"**, which I will speak further about later in this manuscript. This time I would be prepared within my Being, fully able to remain in my Heavenly Home without the presence of unfinished business once, and forever more. My life now experienced that a Celestial and Heavenly door or portal had now opened, that was not present or accessible to me before. If it wasn't for the Loving bond I so cherish with my **devoted wife Suzanna**, I may well have decided it was time to leave this world again, and enter through the portal gates of death, back into one of the **"Twelve Heavenly Realms or Communities"**, I had visited during my NDE. This reawakened desire to become deceased from my physical form and material life, so I could stay permanently in my; **"Afterlife's Celestial Existence"**, now became the new all-consuming challenge for me. In other words, I wanted to die again, so that I could go back to my Heavenly Home and the life, I had so deeply longed for over the many subsequent and prevailing years during this lifetime. Since my beloved Mother's passing, this was a desire that became ever stronger and that I had become more familiar with, on a daily basis. Now that I seemed to be ever more present in the Afterlife than anywhere else, I realized that a part of me never truly returned to my life that had been restored here on earth. My memory of the Afterlife continues to beckon me to return, unto this very day. My life now became one of straddling two worlds simultaneously. A justification for Being in this life, and the pull to return to the part of me still existing and beckoning me from my Afterlife. Yes, it's an ongoing struggle in the living of this life from day to day. Perhaps this would explain why I would have to encounter an additional NDE episode during a horrific car crash in Benson Arizona, just five years following my early childhood NDE drowning. I more fully describe this extraterrestrial experience along with one hundred other short Spiritual Stories, in a future **publication due out in 2017** entitled; **"A Day in the Life"** (*One hundred and one Spiritual Soul Stories of my, so called Life on earth*).

I have been able, with the help of my beloved wife and life time partner both here, and in the Hereafter, to combat

146

the waking state hour's desire to unwittingly create new circumstances to enable another NDE to occur. I certainly don't want to sabotage the Life and Love lessons, that still remain for me to fulfill in this earthly life. It is in my dream time, engaging my most powerful NDE recollections, that I continue to try to stand outside of and apart from, these NDE recurring reflections, as an observer. This NDE replay always seems to occur much more prominently during my NDE Anniversary month of August each year. These dreams are always ever more vivid in their colors and experiential content during this month, than any other month of the year. Often in these dreams, I once again observe replaying scenes from my drowning NDE, but instead of returning to my family parked on the beach, I would often find myself walking along my adolescent neighborhood's, block of homes. Without any pre-meditation my body would be lifted up, and above the homes and tree tops that bordered along my hometown street. I would be floating effortlessly forward looking in, and through the roof tops of the houses below, watching people moving about, going through their daily activities, running around in circles and all played out, in their little living cubicles. It kind of freaked me out at first, observing the smallness and repetition of human existence. But after having so many of these dreams over the years, I simply accepted that they were really just ascended and transcendental visions, or what I have since referred to as; **"Over Soul Observations"**. My "Heaven Seven Guardians" would occasionally whisper the words; **"Above bodies, above minds"**, at such times.

I would be watching people, places, and things, from an overview range of some twenty to thirty feet in distance floating above all such things, appearing just below me. For a time, the dreams just repeated themselves and so were accepted as Being normal, and the usual overnight expected programming for me. Then one night during the Anniversary month of August, the dreams extended into my NDE episode, where I would begin to see those same "Strings of Light", generating themselves from the Sun, that I had originally seen during my drowning NDE. These were the very same Light Strings, I had seen which so brightly glowed around the mouths and nostrils of every person, and life form present. Since these dreams would take place primarily during the early hours of the morning, these Strings of Light would invite me into a separate reality of a Light world, which transformed its earthly inhabitants into, what I have since described as; **"Solarized Light Bodies"**. Years later I would think of these "Solarized Light Body Observations" to be a reflection of what the **Resurrection through the Transformational Light of Jesus Christ**, may have looked like. I so longed at all such times to witness Christ's Resurrection in person. Along with my NDE episode, I kept these visions and thoughts to myself and deeply hidden within. During the course of my earthly waking state time, I knew these personal experiences would be perceived as Being rather odd, and perhaps a bit too eccentric for others to understand. I suppose I thought and felt my extra-terrestrial visitations, would not ever be available for proper comprehension without some prejudice and perhaps a bit of confusion, by others. Somehow, I managed to keep all such things almost a complete secret for some fifty years until I received the guidance from "The Heaven Seven", to complete the publication of this manuscript.

I kept a Personal Diary for much of my life since moving out of my Parent's home at the age of nineteen. I thought it to be the only way I could reflect upon the many metaphysical and paranormal experiences, I had to somehow reconcile and normalize, during the course of my lifetime. My Diary allowed me to chronicle these nether worldly experiences, while keeping them private, for my eyes only. In this way I maintained a record of my lifetime occurrences. Writing in my Personal Diary then became like talking to the friend, which I could never seem to find in my real-time existence. It became an extended written and secret recording, which spoke to me during the many externalized moments of dealing with all my many earthly endeavors. Within the pages of my Diary I could talk to, and ponder some of the deeper meanings of my mystical and meta-physical experiences I so needed to find some reasonable and tangible expression for. Ultimately the relationship I formed with my Diary, allowed me to enter a separate reality radically contrasting itself from what I struggled to make into a more normalized presence in my own daily existence. Throughout the years, my Diary became increasingly more important to me as I spoke with it, as if it was a personal friend, perhaps even like a family member, I could trust and confide my thoughts and feelings with. I may have even superseded my need for personal human relationships because of the Diary. I had been alone for so many years of my life, and I truly loved those years of solitude and the "**Inner Sanctuary**", I had created within and for my own required, "**Peace of Mind**".

My thoughts and lifetime experiences were finding their fullest expression through the silent spaces I had discovered, while writing in my Diary. In this place there was no rebounding commentary, rejection, confusion, or negative criticism to be endured. Perhaps it had stemmed from the fear of Being abandoned again as an infant, at eleven months of age. Whatever it ultimately represented, I knew I needed someone I could share such things with, in an open and honest manner. I could always go back then to read my Diary's entrees, and remember those things which would remain untold, to any other living Soul. At such times as these, I would be randomly reminded by "The Heaven Seven" that, I was a member of what they had called, a **"Soul Group"**. A collection of Souls who were bonded and traveling together during the course of a lifetime, and remained enjoined together as a; **"Spiritual Family"**, from lifetime to lifetime. Yes, they said from **lifetime to lifetime.** I could not seem to get them to explain this to me. Did they mean that we as humans go through **multiple lifetimes** such as is the case with **"Reincarnation..?"** or did it refer to an incarnation here on earth followed by our **Reincarnation into the Afterlife..?** As of yet, I do not know. What I do know from my interactions with "The Heaven Seven" is that one's desires, drive one's lifetime journey and material world experiences. Desire over time then, may be called a Longing. It is this desire or longing which determines the direction and intentions of one's Thoughts, Words, and Deeds in this life, and as such there can be no accidents in life, but only the immediate or delayed effects of desires manifesting themselves in both conscious and un-conscious ways. So each one may need to be careful what you want, what you say, and what you wish for. It all just may come true, even at times in which you may not wish for such things that had once been wished for, to be made manifest and make their unscheduled appearances, during one's ongoing lifetime Love lessons as expressed in all of life's situations, circumstances and impending outcomes.

150

Along with my precious **Diary writings**, which I had dutifully entered on a daily basis, I also found that I was writing and **composing more Prayers and Poems.** These I often dedicated to "The Heaven Seven", and they let me know they received them by increasing the heat of the Sacred Flame I could feel glowing, within my Heart. These transcendental moments only expanded with a greater sincerity and spontaneity, as time future unfolded. I would find that a specific word or words would each project their individual imagery, like a series of word pictures, within my mind. I repeated these words as I continued to visualize; "The Sacred Heart of Jesus Christ", "The Sacred Heart of Mother Mary", and, "The Sacred Hearts of The Holy Family". Just by saying or thinking the words; **"Jesus Christ",** **"Sacred Heart", "Mother Mary",** or **"Holy Family",** a great comfort would come over and consume me for days on end. To think of and speak the names of any of **"The Saints"** became a very personal and sacred ritual which I felt a particular intimacy with during the month of August, and especially on my **August 28th, Anniversary date.**

I would invite anyone who wishes to share in a; **"Prayerful Contemplative Time",** to join with me at **Noon this coming Sunday,** or on any Sunday or week day, as you are guided. I have come to refer to these Sundays in all my messages and posts for many years now as; **"Sacred Sundays".** My particular ritual includes; "**Lighting a Candle**", in a quiet and solitary place, and reciting the following **"Healing Prayer",** which is an adaptation of a prayer originally penned by **James Dillet Freeman;**

151

The Light of God Surrounds Me.
The Love of God Enfolds Me.
The Power of God Protects Me.
The Presence of God Watches over Me.
Wherever I Am... God Is...
God Is Love.♥

I will repeat this prayer multiple times, until my mind is more totally focused on the meaning of the words, and their Spiritual intentions. After proclaiming the Prayer either mentally or aloud, I will sit silently for up to an hour simply following and listening to the movement and expansion of my breathing, with my total focus Being on **taking one concentrated breath at a time**. This entire practice may take anywhere from thirty to sixty minutes, after which if I am not already there, I will go to the **nearest Beach** or **place in Nature**, where I may find any body of water. If you wish to share any of these Spiritual exercises with me, and you're not in close proximity to a body of water, then any place in Nature, will do. This may include a quiet place at a park, pond, river, or water stream. The idea is to **create a "Sacred Environment for your Prayer Time"**. If travel options are not available, then sitting by a tree, bush, or flowers in your own back yard, will work as well. Being close to anything in Nature is helpful in empowering a quiet, focused, contemplative atmosphere, making your Sacred Time more meaningful and Spiritually more, memory indelible. My personal rituals will also include; **floating my body on top of the water** in gentle waves, while feeling the over-riding air currents which flow above the Ocean's surface, gliding upon and across the surface of my body. My eyes may be open or closed, depending on the environment around me. I listen to the sound of my breathing coinciding with the rhythm of the Ocean Surf, **synchronizing itself with the palpitation, of my Heart beats**. I often spend an entire afternoon in the water simply floating upright, with my arms and legs outstretched in a fully surrendered and receptive formation.

If the Sun is shining above, I may open my eyes to a narrow eyelid glimpse, and observe the **beams of Sunlight, streaming in and through my eyes**. In this way I absorb the Sun's own direct illumination, which I allow to enter into my body, mind, Heart, and Soul. After whatever Sacred Hours of time may be desired, granted, and arranged, I will return to my home and position my body in close proximity to the many; **"Temple Altars of Adoration"**, I have co-created in our home with my **"Beloved Lifetime Partner"** and **"Soul Mate, Suzanna"**. This becomes a pre-arranged time of prayerful practice in a prayerfully created place that I think of as; **"Sacred Environmental Compliance"**. This special place in a home then becomes your own; **"Sacred Home Temple Space"**. I will then sit or lie quietly, next to one of our many dedicated Altars, Light all the candles present, and conclude my day in silence, contemplation, adoration, and gratefulness to the; "Higher Power" or, "Holy Spirit", for all of its daily care and guidance in my life. In this way, I am fulfilling the purpose of my life or what I have coined as; **"My Soul, Role, Goal'**. I take special care to create this "Sacred Time" on our **"Designated Day of Rest"** which I refer to as our; "**Sacred Sunday, Day of Worship**". The Prayer I most commonly recite, during my daily and Sacred Sunday Contemplations, I will state as an affirmation either mentally or verbally out loud as follows;

153

"With each and every breath I take,
I fill my body with the healing power of The Holy Spirit
So that I may be a blessing to myself,
and all whose paths I cross...
I pray these special intentions through
the Holy Fire radiating forth,
from the Sacred Heart of Jesus Christ...
God Bless,
(say: your name, your partner's name,
or desired family members name, if applicable)
here... and in the Hereafter..."

Contemplation #08:
*"All former fears, worries,
and every concern...
Were all consumed, in a Sacred Fire,
that did not burn..."*

About the Author

Michael William AngelOh lives on the Northshore of Oahu Hawaii, and has lived in the Hawaiian Islands for thirty-five years. Michael taught Yoga, Meditation and classes in the Healing Arts for some ten years at; **San Jose State University, San Jose City College,** and throughout the Bay Area of California during the 1970's under the pseudonyms; **Michael OmSurya,** and **Michael Sunsurya.** During that time, he had authored four books on various subjects regarding; **Yoga, Meditation, Acupressure Massage and Color Light Conduction.** This will be Michael's first Internationally distributed publication on the subject of his **Near Death Experience** or **NDE** which fortuitously occurred on; **August 28, 1966.** This year celebrates his NDE's **50th Anniversary,** which he simply refers to as; **"0828".**

Michael is also a Music Composer and has produced a number of Hawaiian Music Albums which were distributed by the Music Marketing and Distribution company; **Sunstar Productions**. This company which was co-conceived in 1981, became a major International force in introducing; **"Alternative and Hawaiian Music"** as well as the; **"Touch Pad Music Listening Stations"**, featured in over one hundred high-traffic Resort locations throughout the State of Hawaii and in many top National tourism and Resort communities throughout the United States. He co-founded and incorporated Sunstar Productions on the island of Maui Hawaii, with his long time and devoted business partner; **Antoinette Kehaulani Pahia.**

Michael composed and produced his first domestic digital Music Album release under the new Music genre he has coined as; **"Devotional Fusion Music"**. His latest Music Album entitled; **"Sacred Hearts Afire"**, is his first new CD Album production in some twenty years. Currently posted at #3 on the; **"Inspirational Music Charts"**, it features Songs written and adapted from classic Biblical Scriptures including the title track; **"The Lord's Prayer"**. The Album's Music tracks then offer seventeen Inspirational Song selections, presenting the listener with every opportunity to grow their own; **Sacred Heart, State of Being.** These days Michael still lives in beautiful Hawaii with his beloved **wife and lifetime partner Suzanna AngelOh.** He publishes his weekly; **"Hawaiian Words of Wisdom"** and, **"Sacred Sunday Words of Wisdom"**, on multiple Social Media platforms and writes somewhat seclusively about; **Hawaiian Island Life, Christian Mysticism, Spiritual Ascension** and the **Global Healing Arts.**

Mahalo nui loa, Thank you kindly...
Ke Akua me ke Aloha, May God Bless You... ♥

Watch my **YouTube Music Video** featuring the first Track; **"The Lord's Prayer"** from the CD Music Album; "**Sacred Hearts Afire**" here:
»-<♥>-» https://youtu.be/ckjnREuXxIQ
Graphic Designs by Lisa Arts: https://www.fiverr.com/lisaarts
Contact Michael William AngelOh:
beautiful-dreamer-publications@1800sunstar.com
Michael William AngelOh Blog: https://michael-william-angeloh.blogspot.com/

Made in the USA
Columbia, SC
04 March 2019